Bullseye Success Guides

BIRDWATCHING

Galley Press

Authors: Steve Madge and
Catherine Dell

Adviser: Michael Chinery

Editor: Frances Ferneyhough

Cover design: John Strange

Copyright © 1983 by Grisewood & Dempsey Ltd.

Published in 1987 in this edition by Galley Press,
an imprint of W.H. Smith and Son Limited,
Registered No. 237811 England. Trading as
W.H. Smith Distributors, St John's House,
East Street, Leicester LE1 6NE

ISBN 0 86136 627 1

Printed and bound in Italy by Vallardi Industrie Grafiche

Contents

An Interest for Everyone

Look out of the window. Almost certainly you will see some birds – pigeons crossing a city street, starlings digging up the lawn, sparrows pecking greedily at a crust of bread, swallows perched on an overhead cable. There are birds everywhere: in towns and cities, in fields and forests, on moors and mountains, in gardens and parks, by rivers and seashores. And because birds live in all kinds of places (and because there are many kinds of birds) watching birds has become a very popular hobby.

It is easy to begin birdwatching: all you need is a good pair of eyes! You may choose to start by observing the birds in your garden or by looking out for birds on the way to school. With the help of a good reference book – or a bird-expert friend – you will soon recognize common, everyday species like blackbirds and blue tits. Then you may become so interested that you want to learn more about birds. How do they fly? Why do they sing? What are the differences between birds that live in marshes and ones that live on mountains? You can find the answers to these questions in books, but it is even more exciting to discover the bird world first-hand – as a birdwatcher.

Birdwatching is the type of hobby that suits everyone. You can make it as simple or as complicated as you like. At one end of the scale, birdwatching means just noticing which birds visit the garden; at the other end, it means hours of patient observation, visits to nature reserves, and using special equipment such as binoculars, telescopes, tape recorders and cameras.

As people become more and more involved in birdwatching, they sometimes decide to specialize. They may choose to study one bird in particular, or to concentrate on the birds of a specific habitat (such as mountain, lake, woodland, or town). Or they may select some aspect of bird life such as feeding, nest-building or migration.

This book introduces you to birdwatching: what you need, where to go, how to observe. It also contains background information on birds so that you know what to look for and can then understand what you see. Happy birdwatching!

Opposite: Next time you see a robin in a garden or park, have a good look. How long is it? What colour are its tail and wings? What shape feet has it got? Does it eat seeds or insects? Listen to its song: just one note or several? After a few minutes you will have discovered quite a lot about the robin – and you will have had your first try at birdwatching.

Many birdwatchers like to keep lists of the different kinds of birds they have seen, and the dates on which they have spotted them. Even a list of birds in your own garden can be interesting; you could keep it in the form of a diary. Noting the days on which you see the first arrival of summer migrants is a good idea; you can compare one year with another. And your lists can be helpful; ornithology is one of the few sciences which relies on amateur help. Most data is collected by enthusiastic birdwatchers out in the field, not by professional scientists.

What you Need

A group of young birdwatchers can learn a lot with adult help, and most people love to share their knowledge. Binoculars are essential equipment, but even small ones feel heavy after a time and holding them up to the eyes becomes tiring. Always carry binoculars on a strap round your neck; they will be ready when you want to use them, and safe just in case you drop them.

Birdwatchers can discover a lot about birds by just using their eyes and remembering what they have seen, but they get even more enjoyment from their hobby if they have – and use – some basic equipment.

Starter kit
For beginners, this basic equipment is not expensive: a notebook, a pencil and a bird recognition book (which can be borrowed from a library).

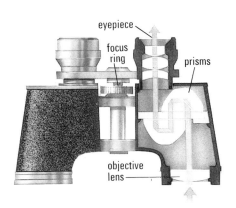

eyepiece

focus ring

prisms

objective lens

Most binoculars are prismatic. This means that they contain prisms to reflect the light inside so that they can be made small and portable. When the ring is turned the eyepieces move in or out to focus the image. Binoculars come in a wide range of prices. Cheaper makes are often adequate for birdwatching purposes but the more expensive ones are stronger and damp-proof and should last a lifetime. When buying binoculars, always test them: focus on a distant object and then on something close up.

Ideally, the notebook should be pocket-sized. To stop its pages flapping in the wind, hold them together with a strong rubber band; the rubber band will also grip the pencil when not in use. A pencil is more convenient than a ball-point pen because it is easier to use in damp weather; but remember to take a sharpener or penknife with you in case the point breaks or becomes blunt. Birdwatchers use their notebooks all the time, jotting down anything of interest they see and hear. Sometimes they draw quick pictures to remind them of what they are looking at. Then, when they get home, they write out proper records from their notes and check their observations in bird books. (For more information on records see page 15.)

Extra eyes

Most birds are easily frightened and fly away if people try to approach them. So, for a close-up view of birds, binoculars are essential.

There are many kinds of binoculars, but not all are suitable for birdwatching. Every pair of binoculars is marked with a set of figures: for example, 8×40. The first number is the magnifying power; the bird appears eight times ($8 \times$) bigger than it really is. The second number is the diameter in millimetres (40 mm) of the objective lens – the big lens farthest from the eyepiece. A large diameter gives a brighter image and a wider field of view (what you can see). Big lenses, however, make the binoculars heavy and bulky and tiring to carry; also, if the magnification is too high, the image dances as your hand shakes. So it

> **WARNING**
> NEVER look directly at the Sun through binoculars or a telescope. This can make you blind.

Telescopes have much higher magnification powers than binoculars, which make them very suitable for identifying birds at a distance. However, high magnifications exaggerate the user's movements – even the slightest ones caused by breathing – and as a result the image shakes. For a steady picture, the telescope must be mounted on a tripod.

is best to choose binoculars with a medium specification: not smaller than 7×30, not bigger than 10×50.

To observe distant birds in detail – like sea birds on the horizon or migrating flocks overhead – you will need to use a telescope. Telescopes give much higher magnification than binoculars (up to $60 \times$) but they are awkward to carry and quite difficult to focus. When in use, a telescope must be fixed to a tripod, or held steady on a wall, to prevent the image shaking.

On film

As well as keeping written records, many bird-watchers like to take photographs of the areas they visit and the birds they see. For general landscape and habitat pictures (such as lake-sides, gardens and hedgerows) a fixed-lens camera is adequate. But for close-up shots of birds, use a camera that accepts various lenses, including a telephoto lens; a SLR (single-lens-reflex) camera is best. The most useful telephoto lenses are from 300 mm (which magnifies about 5 times) to 500 mm (about 9 times).

Bird photographers generally use 35 mm film, either black-and-white or colour transparency. As

Above: A SLR (single-lens-reflex) camera that accepts interchangeable lenses is ideal for bird photography.
Below: For close-up shots of birds, a telephoto lens of not less than 300 mm is essential.

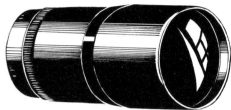

Below: A tripod to keep the camera steady. This is necessary when using a high-powered telephoto lens as the greater the magnification, the greater the amount of 'shake'. For really sharp pictures, fast films (ASA 200 or more) should be used with shutter speeds of between 1/250 and 1/1000.

This photograph of two Canada geese and goslings was not difficult to take. It is the sort of scene easily found in a local park with a lake, where the birds are tame enough to come quite close. It was taken with a single-lens-reflex camera with a 200 mm lens; the speed of the shutter was 1/125 second and the aperture of the diaphragm f.8. If the birds had been swimming fast, or if the wind had caused quick-moving ripples on the water, a higher shutter speed would have been necessary.

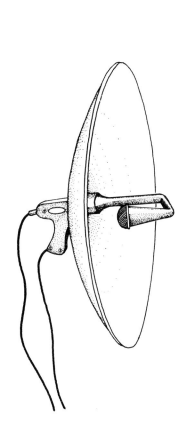

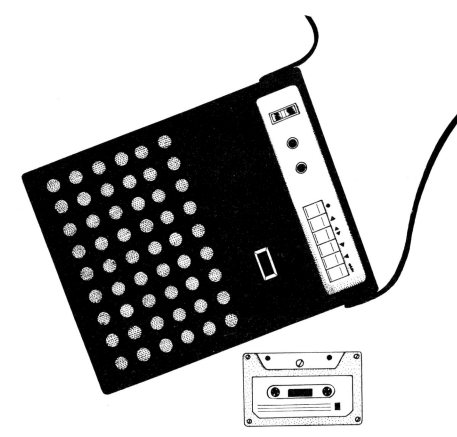

Above: Birdwatchers often use a parabolic reflector when recording songs and calls. The reflector, a wide bowl with a microphone at its centre, is aimed at the bird. It concentrates the sound waves into the centre of the bowl and into the microphone which, as you can see, points towards the centre of the bowl and not towards the bird.

Right: A portable cassette tape recorder is very useful in the field. The birdwatcher can use it to record songs and calls and to make verbal notes.

fast shutter speeds have to be used (to 'freeze' the birds, especially in flight), the film itself should be high-speed. Films rated from ASA 200/DIN 24 to ASA 400/DIN 27 are ideal for the birdwatcher's purpose.

Photographing birds is not easy as they fly away at the slightest sound or movement. So it is a good idea to practise on something simple before taking your camera on field trips. Try making a study of garden birds round the birdtable or visit the park and focus on a group of pigeons or ducks. Never try to photograph birds on their nests. You will disturb and frighten them and may even cause parent birds to desert. (And unless you are an expert photographer, the results will be poor.) The photographs of nesting birds in this book have been taken by experts with great experience.

On tape
A small tape recorder is another useful item of birdwatching equipment. It is handy for dictating on-the-spot descriptions of birds and invaluable for recording songs and calls. The inexpensive light-weight type can produce excellent recordings, provided a good quality microphone is used; the type of microphone normally supplied with a portable recorder is not suitable for outdoor work, especially on windy days. As with photography, it is a good idea to practise first on garden birds. Try recording the robin's clear call or the non-stop chatter of starlings.

Although these birdwatchers are walking carefully and are partly hidden by undergrowth and bushes, their blue clothing is rather bright and conspicuous. The best colours for camouflage are dull shades of grey, brown and green.

Dressing up

Birdwatchers often find themselves out in the rain, wind and cold and, as they have to stay still and quiet, they cannot keep warm by rushing about. For this reason, clothing must be warm and waterproof. It should include a jacket or anorak made of hardwearing, rainproof material (but not nylon or similar man-made fibres that rustle with every movement); choose a jacket which has several large pockets for carrying your notebook and other items and which also has a hood. Hoods and floppy hats break up the outline of the head and shoulders; the human shape is well known to birds and they usually avoid it. Stout walking boots, worn with two pairs of thick wool socks, are warmer than Wellington boots and mittens are warmer than gloves; but it is difficult to operate binoculars and cameras wearing mittens. Fingerless gloves are good if the weather is not too cold.

Disguise

Birds see people as enemies, so if you want to get near them you must make yourself as invisible as possible. This means wearing camouflage colours – dull greens, browns and greys – that disappear into the background. Army-type combat jackets in patchy shades of green and brown are ideal.

Birds do not trust people, so birdwatchers must try to make themselves unnoticeable by wearing dull colours. This is especially true in flat open countryside where there is no natural cover such as bushes, trees and banks to hide the birdwatcher.

Keeping a Record

Keeping a record adds interest to birdwatching. And, as times goes by and you become more experienced, your notes could be useful to local and national wildlife organizations. You might, for example, discover a link between the feeding habitats of certain birds and pollution from a nearby factory.

In the field

When you are out birdwatching, it is far better to make too many notes than too few. You can always leave unimportant details out of your permanent record, but you cannot add what you no longer remember.

To begin with, always note the time, date, weather conditions and habitat. When it comes to the bird itself, describe its size and shape (compare it with a similar, known bird), its bill and feet, plumage colours and patterns; also include the bird's habits like feeding, flight and song.

Try to make a rough sketch and label any distinguishing features such as bill shape and wing markings. Drawing a bird is not difficult: make a large oval for the body and a smaller one for the head; join them with the neck and then add wings, tail, bill, legs and feet.

Identification

If you see an unfamiliar bird you will have to try to identify it by checking your notes against a bird recognition book. Sometimes the illustration in the book does not seem quite right but the text alongside may clear up doubts. Many people like to have at least two recognition books to get as much help as possible.

At home

There are several ways of arranging records. One of the most popular methods is in the form of a diary. Another is to enter observations under species headings such as 'blackbird', 'wren', 'sparrow'; in this case it is best to use a loose-leaf book so that you can add extra pages as necessary. But however you arrange your notes it is essential to number the pages and make a good index, preferably on cards so that you can easily add to it.

In the field, birdwatchers make notes of everything they see and hear. If they spot an unfamiliar bird they can look it up later in a reference book, using their notes as a guide.

A rough sketch of a bird with labels for colours, markings, bill shape, etc is often more helpful for identification purposes than a long written description.

What to Look For

Is that large black bird, perched alone on a fence post, a rook or a crow? And is that speed-ace, twisting and turning in the air, a swallow or a house martin? How do we know which bird is which?

Bird identification is not really difficult as there are all kinds of clues – clues like size, shape, plumage, markings, bill, feet, behaviour, calls and habitat. At a glance, two separate species may look alike, but if you study them closely you will discover a difference. Take rooks and crows: they are both largish, black birds but crows are normally seen alone or in pairs, while rooks are sociable and live in large groups. And when it comes to swallows and house martins, the swallow's throat is red, the martin's is white and the swallow's tail is more forked.

The beginner's first task is to recognize common birds. Once an observer knows familiar species, he or she can use them as a guide for describing unfamiliar birds. For example, is the mystery bird's beak short and stout like a sparrow's or thin and pointed like a starling's? Does it have a stubby, upturned tail like a wren or a long, straight one like a wagtail?

As birdwatchers gain experience, they find it easier to identify new birds and also to recognize familiar birds from their flight and song.

Above: Willow warblers at their nest in a bush. Willow warblers belong to the same family as chiffchaffs and, to look at, the two species are almost identical. But they can be distinguished by their voices: the willow warbler has a musical song of descending notes, while the chiffchaff has a monotonous two-note song. Also, the willow warbler likes thick undergrowth and bushes, while the chiffchaff prefers trees.

Opposite: Some birds have distinctive wing markings which help identification. The chaffinch, for instance, can always be recognized by its two startling white wing bars.

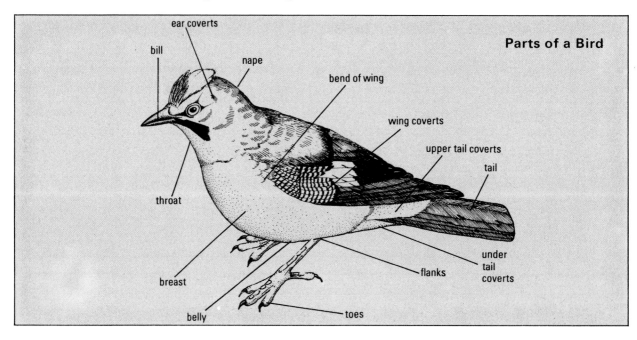

Parts of a Bird

ear coverts
bill
nape
bend of wing
wing coverts
upper tail coverts
tail
throat
under tail coverts
flanks
breast
belly
toes

Birds are sometimes forced to change their habitat. Traditionally, oystercatchers, like this one, nest on the beach. But as more and more holidaymakers spend summer by the sea, there is less and less room for oystercatchers. As a result, the birds have moved inland and now breed on open moors and by lakes and rivers.

The familiar colourings of birds in illustrations can be misleading, for these often show only the male bird in its brightly coloured breeding plumage. Many birds, such as the turnstone (below, top) have one pattern of colours in summer (right) and another in winter (left). In some birds, like the goldfinch (below, centre) the young birds (left) have a different pattern of colours from the adult birds (right). And in many birds, such as the mallard ducks (bottom), the male (right) and female (left) have different colours. So shape is the best guide, using colour to back it up.

Habitat

Different birds belong to different places. Some, like gulls and gannets, live by the sea; others, such as owls and finches, prefer woods and forests. These 'home areas' are called habitats and the main ones are farmland, woods, heathland, moors, mountains, lakes, rivers, marshes, coasts, estuaries, gardens and towns.

All these habitats can be sub-divided. Woodlands, for instance, break down into coniferous and broad-leaved (mostly deciduous) and both types have their own bird life. Crossbills, goldcrests and goshawks are three of the species found in coniferous forests while broad-leaved woods provide a home for nuthatches, tawny owls, woodpeckers, jays and many others.

A bird's habitat is a useful clue to its identity. If you see what looks like a blackbird on a barren moor you are probably watching a ring ouzel; but if you find a ring ouzel nesting in the garden hedge, it is certainly a blackbird.

Some birds have two habitats: one for nesting and one for winter feeding. The lapwing, for example, breeds inland – on moors and in fields – but often spends the winter along the coast, probing the mud for worms, grubs and shellfish.

Male ruffs are unmistakable in the breeding season when they grow a broad coloured collar (ruff). But in winter, they are less easy to identify. They vary in length from 18 cm to 30 cm; their underparts may be whitish or fawn and their legs anything from black to orange-red. All ruffs, however, have a distinctive head shape – small and rounded.

The silhouettes of these common birds show that each species has a distinct shape. Notice the duck's rounded crown and the woodpecker's flat one; compare the heron's long graceful neck with the owl's; and see how the robin has thin legs and the duck much thicker ones.

Shape

A bird has a definite shape. Try to get a good view of several different birds on the ground: maybe a pigeon, starling and sparrow. If you look carefully, you will see that each one has its own shape. For example, the body, legs and neck may be fat, thin, short or long and the top of the head, the crown, could be flat or rounded.

Learning to recognize species by their shape is useful. It helps you to identify birds when they are against the sun or so far away that you cannot see other features or colours. It also helps you to distinguish between species that are otherwise quite similar.

Size

A bird's size is another important clue to its identity. Often, two species appear almost identical: the whooper swan and Bewick's swan are very alike but the whooper is larger.

Bird books usually give measurements. Although these are not much help in the field (it is hard to tell whether the bird you are watching is 19 cm or 20 cm long) they are useful for making comparisons. If you are observing an unfamiliar bird and think it is about the same size as a blackbird, you can look up a blackbird's details and then try to identify the new bird from its length as well as from colour, shape and habits.

Bird Shapes

duck

heron

robin

finch

owl

woodpecker

Plumage

The first thing people usually notice about a bird is its plumage – its covering of feathers. As well as noting the overall colour, look out for patterns and markings. Is there a general pattern – perhaps striped or mottled? Are there any wing markings? What about the tail, rump and face?

Plumage patterns are often linked to habitat and lifestyle. Many birds that flock together in open spaces have white markings; these act as alarm signals. If, for example, a flock of chaffinches is feeding on the ground and one bird takes fright and flies off, its white wing and tail flashes immediately warn the others that something is wrong. Plumage colour also serves as camouflage, hiding the bird from enemies. The woodcock, dark and speckled, is invisible among dead leaves.

When noting plumage for identification purposes, remember that colours can vary according to sex and age. In many species, females are duller than males. The female's drab plumage camouflages her when she is sitting on the nest, while the male's handsome colours help him to attract a mate. Young birds, too, are quite drab; even males do not acquire their full colour until they are ready for breeding. The young goldfinch, for instance, has no crimson on its face and only a pale wing bar.

Some species even have two plumages: one for winter and one for the breeding season. Various members of the sandpiper family, for example, are grey-brown in winter but reddish in summer. The ptarmigan changes from brown and white in summer to white in winter to camouflage it against the snow.

This flock of sandwich terns includes both adult and juvenile birds. The adults are whitish-grey with black crowns, while the young birds have dark mottled wings.

When the black-headed gull moults, it loses its dark hood and acquires whitish head plumage for winter. But a bit of the hood remains as a collar round the neck. In this state it looks like a Ross's gull which has a black neck collar during the breeding season.

Guillemots, like most seabirds, have a two-tone dark and white plumage. When they are in the water, their dark backs blend with the colour of the waves, while from below, their pale underparts are mistaken by fish for the sky.

Above: The dunlin, a typical wader, has a long slender bill which it uses to probe deep into the mud, searching for tiny creatures.

Above right: A bird's bill suits its feeding habits. Herons have long powerful beaks for spearing fish. The kestrel, like other birds of prey, uses its fierce hooked bill to tear animal flesh apart. Blue tits hammer at seeds and nuts with their small stout beaks. Blackbirds have quite stout all-purpose beaks for stabbing into fruit as well as digging for worms. The avocet's long curved bill skims creatures off the water surface. Tree creepers dig out insects from tree bark with their thin curved beaks.

Bill Shapes

heron

kestrel

blue tit

tree creeper

blackbird

avocet

Beaks

The shape of a bird's beak, or bill, is related to its feeding methods. By recognizing basic beak types, birdwatchers can guess at habitat and diet – important clues for identification.

Birds of prey, from eagles to owls, have hooked bills for tearing flesh. Fishing birds, like divers and grebes, use spear-like beaks to stab and hold fish. Sandpipers, curlews and other waders probe into the mud with long, slender bills. Ducks and swans need broad, flat beaks with which they can sift plant food from water. Short, stout bills belong to seed-eaters such as finches while insect-eaters, like warblers, have slim bills.

The puffin's large colourful bill has saw-tooth edges so that it can hold several fish at once.

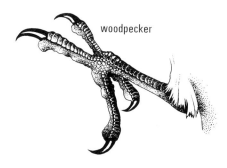

woodpecker

Left and above: Woodpeckers must grip a tree-trunk very firmly while they drill into it. To help them do this they have two forward toes, and two backward ones; they also use their tails for extra support.

Below: Four different types of feet. The eagle's foot is strong and muscular with sharp claws, or talons, for grasping prey. A perching bird has multi-purpose feet that can run, hop and cling to branches. The duck's webbed foot and the grebe's lobed foot are both ideal for swimming.

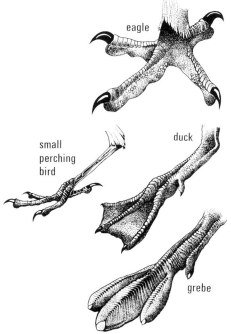

eagle

small perching bird

duck

grebe

Feet

Birds live in all kinds of places: on the ground, up trees, by the sea, among rocks, and in rivers. But whatever their particular habitat may be they have specially designed feet to help them survive in it. There are several basic types of feet (but not as many as beaks) and, as they are a vital part of the bird, the observer should learn to recognize them.

All birds, except the ostrich, have four toes. In most species, these are arranged three forward and one backwards. But a few birds, like cuckoos and woodpeckers, have two pointing each way. Ospreys and owls, both birds of prey, are able to move one front toe backwards or forwards as they please. (Ostriches are unique in having only two toes.)

The great family of perching birds, which includes many woodland species and others that like to hop around on the ground, has slender, well-developed toes. The three forward, one backward arrangement makes it easy for them to grasp twigs and branches. Birds of prey use their feet to seize and kill their victims. Their toes are equipped with powerful claws and strong muscles. The osprey, which feeds on live fish, has rough, spiny toes for grasping and carrying its slippery supper.

Waterbirds have very special feet. Webs of skin connect the main toes so that they form paddles for swimming and diving. On the forward stroke, webs and toes are folded, offering little resistance to the water; on the back stroke, the whole foot is spread out to propel the bird along.

The coot, like the grebe, has superefficient swimming feet. Instead of having connected webs, the bird's toes have separate lobes that open as the feet push back against the water then close as they come forward again. But although this type of foot is very powerful underwater, it is quite clumsy on land.

Flight

When birds are flying way up in the sky, identification becomes much more difficult. They are often too distant for birdwatchers to distinguish features like wing markings, beak length and head size. Instead, they must be recognized by the way they fly and by their shape in the air (quite different from their shape on the ground).

When studying a bird's flight, there are several points to look for. First is height. Birds move at different heights: swifts and eagles, for example, fly very high; others, like shearwaters and pheasants, are usually seen low down. Then note the wingbeats. Are they very slow like a heron's, stiff like a fulmar's, fluttering like warblers or rapid like auks? And what about the flight movement itself? For example, starlings fly in a straight line; finches and woodpeckers have a wavy flight path; tits move in jerks; skylarks rise straight up; kestrels hover almost motionless.

The outline of a flying bird is also a good clue to its identity. Different types have differing shapes. Many birds of prey, for instance, have strong broad wings for soaring high and circling in the air. Observers should note the size of the wings (thin, broad, short, long), whether they are pointed or rounded at the tips and whether, for soaring, they are held flat or are angled upwards. Notice too how far the feet trail out beyond the tail and how far the head and bill stick out in front.

Songs and calls

If you cannot see a bird clearly, listen to it: the sound that it makes is a sure means of identification. Most

On long-distance journeys some birds fly in formation. Geese, for example, usually fly in a zigzag or V-formation; each bird appears to take advantage of the slack air behind the one in front. The leading bird at the point of the V is regularly replaced. The picture shows snow geese flying in formation.

On their migration flight buzzards make use of warm air currents. They rise with the warm air, glide for a bit and lose height, then pick up another warm air current and rise again. In this way they use their wings very little and so conserve energy.

Opposite: Most birds sing from a special perch like a post or tree branch. But if there are no trees around they often use telegraph wires, as this stonechat is doing.

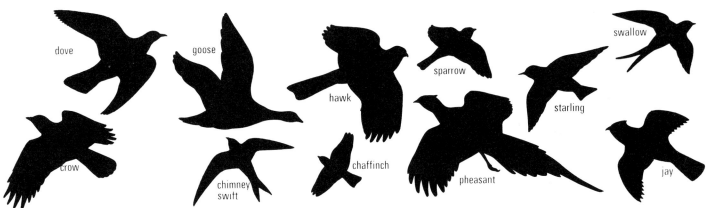

In the air, many birds have unmistakable shapes. The crow and jay belong to the same family and have rounded wings with ragged ends; the dove's wings are broad and pointed; geese have long narrow wings; swifts and swallows have narrow, swept-back wings for fast flight; the starling, too, moves quickly; hawks and other birds of prey have broad wings for soaring; small birds, like chaffinches and sparrows, have short broad wings for changing direction easily; game birds such as pheasants have broad rounded wings for quick take-off (they normally live on the ground and only fly to escape danger).

birds sing only during the breeding season. They start in early spring when they are setting up territory – their own patch for nesting – and continue during the summer. A bird uses its song to attract a mate and to warn off intruders.

Besides song, birds have a range of calls: alarm calls, contact calls and flight calls. Some have as many as 40 different calls.

Learning bird songs and calls is very difficult. The best way is to listen with an experienced birdwatcher who can tell you which bird is making which noise. Records and tape recordings of songs and calls are also helpful.

A strange form of migration takes place among birds which eat only one food, perhaps a particular seed or berry. If it is a bad year and crops of that food fail completely, then the birds leave their normal habitat and invade an area where they are not usually found. Common invasion species, as they are called, include waxwings, crossbills, snowy owls and nutcrackers. The nutcracker shown here comes from the coniferous forests of Siberia; at irregular intervals it is found as far west as England and southern France.

On the Move

In the bird world, winter often brings death. Cold is not the killer; most birds can keep warm by fluffing out their feathers. The killer is starvation. Because winter days are short, there is less time for birds to find food. Then, as the weather grows colder, flying insects disappear. So birds like swallows, that live on flies and midges, have nothing to eat. When it starts to freeze and snow, the situation gets desperate. As lakes and rivers ice over, freshwater birds go hungry.

Many migrants band together to make their long journeys in huge flocks. Some fly in formation; geese make a big V or long line in the sky, and the leading bird regularly changes. Large birds like geese and ducks have a cruising speed between 65 and 100 kph; even small songbirds travel at over 30 kph, and they can keep up such speeds for a long time.

Ringing helps us study migration. Birds like this jack snipe are caught and a numbered ring is fixed to the leg. Later, if the bird is re-captured or found dead, its ring number is noted, together with the date and location. These details are sent to the ringing organization so that a picture of bird movements can be studied. Ringing is a difficult operation and must only be done by trained experts. Jack snipes breed in the far north of Europe, but spend winter in Mediterranean lands and the British Isles.

In early autumn, birds get ready for their long migration flight. Members of the swallow family, like these sand martins, often collect on overhead wires. Because the journey is so hazardous, migrating birds frequently band together and travel in large flocks for safety.

As snow falls on woods and fields, many others must starve to death.

Survival tactics
Many bird species take the same solution to the problem of winter: migration. They escape the snow and ice by flying away to somewhere warmer. Some birds migrate from one continent to another, travelling thousands of kilometres. But others make far shorter journeys. Gulls, for example, often leave the stormy seas and move inland to find shelter and food in towns and farms. And in mountain areas, birds that spend summer among the peaks may spend winter in the valleys.

Long-distance travel
Some birds migrate vast distances. The warblers that breed in Europe escape to North Africa for winter, making a round trip of 4000 kilometres. Swallows, flying from Britain to southern Africa and back, travel at least 16,000 kilometres. The little wheatear's return journey from Greenland to West Africa is even longer. But the record holder for long-distance migration is the Arctic tern: each year this small seabird covers an incredible 30,000 kilometres as it flies to and fro between the Arctic and the Antarctic.

The Artic tern is a champion traveller. This small seabird breeds in northern lands around the Arctic. Each autumn it flies 15,000 kilometres south to spend a second summer in the Antarctic; but it returns to the other end of the Earth the next spring. Because the Arctic tern travels from one land of the midnight summer sun to another, it spends more of its life in daylight than any other living creature.

Ready for take-off

For their flight across oceans and continents, migrating birds need enormous energy. Some species are able to feed as they travel: seabirds dive down to snatch fish from the waves and swallows catch flying insects on the wing. But others have to survive long periods on the wing without food. So, before leaving their breeding grounds, they eat and eat to build up reserves of fat: small birds, like warblers, often double their weight.

Migration always happens at the same time each year and is controlled by the length of daylight. Somehow birds know that shorter days mean less food and that they must leave before supplies run out. As departure day draws near, they gather together in huge flocks and become very restless until, suddenly, they all take off.

Route-finding

Migrating birds find their way partly through instinct and partly by navigation. Species that fly mostly during the day, such as swallows and martins, orientate themselves by the Sun; night travellers, like warblers, use the stars. It is also probable that birds respond to the Earth's magnetic field, as if they had a built-in compass.

Migrants face many dangers: bad weather – especially gale-force winds that blow them off course, long sea-crossings, deserts and mountains. Even light-houses and oil-rig flares are a hazard as they attract night fliers into the glass or flames where many are killed.

The swallow, like the Arctic tern, enjoys two summers every year: one in Europe where it breeds and then, because its migration flight takes it across the Equator, a second summer in southern Africa. Swallows have a phenomenal sense of time and direction. Not only do they arrive back on the same day – or almost – each year, but they also return to the very same nest. This swallow is catching insects from just above the water's surface.

Trafalgar Square is famous for its fountains, its monuments and for the thousands of street pigeons which live there. They spend the day eating crumbs and seeds scattered by tourists, and at night they roost on nearby buildings. In London and many other big cities, street pigeons are a nuisance. Their nests often block drain pipes and ventilators and their droppings foul pavements, annoy pedestrians, spoil paintwork and cause damage, through corrosion, to buildings and statues.

Birds in Towns

Many birds lead a city life. Generations ago their ancestors belonged to the countryside. But as their natural habitats – woods, hedges and fields – were ruthlessly taken over by roads, buildings and people, the birds were forced to look for new places in which to live. Some escaped deeper into the country. Others moved into built-up areas.

The good life

Town birds have two big advantages over their country neighbours: it is easy for them to keep warm and to find food. All large towns and cities are 'heat islands': the numbers of people, traffic and heating systems raise the temperature several degrees. This extra warmth is trapped by the brick, stone and concrete all around. Temperature differences are so

Street pigeons are descended from wild rock doves, which were first domesticated 5000 years or more ago. In early times they were kept for eggs and meat, but by about 2000 BC 'homing' pigeons were being used as messengers, since they will fly home even when they are released more than 1500 kilometres away. In some countries they ran regular postal services, and carried messages in times of war. During the Second World War more than 250,000 pigeons were used by the British and US armies. The same sort of pigeons are still kept for racing.

Over the centuries, food pigeons strayed or were abandoned, while some racers and messengers lost their way. Such birds went back to living wild, yet kept a link with civilization by adopting city streets and squares as home.

Above: Starlings are energetic scavengers but as they mostly feed at ground level, they make easy prey for cats.

Right: House sparrows have lived alongside people for thousands of years and so, quite naturally, followed them into cities.

Below: Many birds adapt this skills to make the most of town life. Blue tits peck through milk bottle tops to reach the cream underneath, while magpies, traditional egg-thieves, will rob doorstep egg cartons of their contents.

great that some species can live in a city but not outside it because of the cold. This is true of the black redstart, found in sunny southern Europe and in the 'heat island' of London!

Towns also provide birds with an endless supply of food: scraps in dustbins and litter baskets, spilled grain in dockland warehouses, and the tonnes of crumbs, seeds and nuts scattered by bird-lovers, especially in winter.

Problems

Although there is plenty of food in towns, there is not much variety. Some species, like insect-eating birds, cannot get the right diet and so prefer to live in the country. Another drawback of city life is the shortage of secure nesting sites safe from cats and egg thieves. Birds that nest low down – on the ground or in bushes – are often in real danger.

The top three

Most city birds – like city people – live in the suburbs and keep away from the centre with its mass of concrete, crowds, cars, dirt and din. But there are three notable exceptions: pigeons, sparrows and starlings.

Street pigeons

The street pigeon is a familiar sight in towns and cities all over the world. In some places, like Trafalgar Square in London and St Mark's Square in Venice, pigeons have even become a tourist attraction. The pigeon's wild relation, the rock dove, lives on cliffs. So does the street pigeon in its own way: from a bird's point of view, buildings are just concrete cliffs with convenient ledges.

Street pigeons come in many colours: white, pink, blue, brown, grey and black, sometimes patterned, sometimes plain. Traditionally, they feed on seeds and grains which they find in nearby parks, flour mills and wasteland. But generally, they live as scavengers pecking at scraps of bread, cake, cheese, sausage, chocolate or even ice cream.

• The street pigeon's nesting habits, like its eating habits, have adapted to city life. Where the rock dove nests in cliff caves and on rock shelves, the street pigeon chooses bridge girders, church towers, window ledges, chimney stacks, ventilators, lofts and attics. The nest itself is not necessarily built of twigs and straw: rusty wire, telephone cable and polythene bags have all been used.

Litter baskets are a popular source of food for scavenging birds. Although the house sparrow has the stout bill of a seed-eater, it has adapted its diet and will eagerly peck at all types of edible garbage.

The house sparrow, 15 cm, always found near people, is streaky brown; the male has a grey crown and black bib. Sparrows nest in buildings and bushes and feed on the ground off seeds and grains.

The starling, 21 cm, has a dark speckled plumage. It struts around, probing the earth for grubs, and chatters constantly; often it mimics other birds. Starlings live in huge flocks in winter.

The street pigeon, 33 cm, has a plump body, small head and short legs; its plumage varies. Street pigeons live in huge flocks and can fly very fast.

Although house martins nest on buildings, they are more often found in suburbs than in city centres. In totally built-up areas, there is little mud for nest construction and few flying insects for food.

House sparrows

House sparrows are completely at home in the city centre where they hop around public squares, demolition sites, railway stations, street markets and even inside large buildings like cathedrals and museums. Bread is their staple food although at breeding time they often supplement this with seeds and insects. House sparrows' nests are rather untidy and tucked in almost anywhere: behind a drain pipe, alongside a loose brick or tucked into a statue's elbow. Unlike most birds, the house sparrow uses its nest throughout the year, sleeping soundly in it on cold winter nights.

Starlings and others

Starlings are very adaptable and will eat almost anything, especially in winter when the earth is too hard to dig for insects and worms. They find holes for their nests in old walls and under eaves. In winter, huge clouds of starlings fill the evening sky as they prepare to roost on city buildings. Some of the flocks are local and some are from surrounding areas, but all want a night's warmth and shelter. As many as 100,000 starlings can roost each night around Trafalgar Square in the centre of London.

Other birds found in town centres include blackbirds, pied wagtails, black-headed gulls, tawny owls and kestrels (there to eat the sparrows). If you happen to see anything else, like a robin, blue tit or thrush, then probably there is a garden or park nearby.

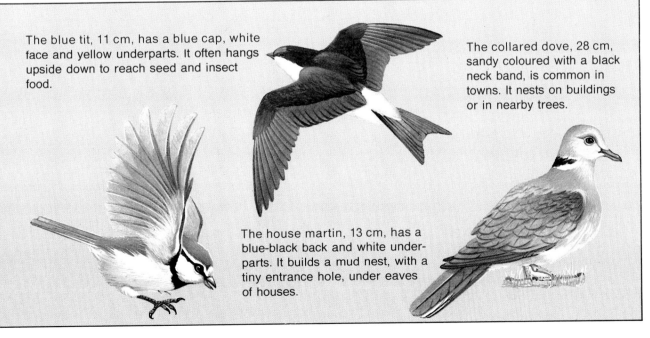

The blue tit, 11 cm, has a blue cap, white face and yellow underparts. It often hangs upside down to reach seed and insect food.

The collared dove, 28 cm, sandy coloured with a black neck band, is common in towns. It nests on buildings or in nearby trees.

The house martin, 13 cm, has a blue-black back and white underparts. It builds a mud nest, with a tiny entrance hole, under eaves of houses.

In the Garden

To many birds, home means a garden. This is especially true in towns. For although some species, like street pigeons and starlings, can survive successfully in city centres, most birds need a more natural environment with at least some greenery: grass, bushes and trees.

Garden birds
Even the smallest garden – just a tiny lawn and a clump of flowers – has some bird life: perhaps a robin, blackbird, dunnock and collared dove. In a larger

Song thrushes like eating snails. When the bird finds a snail it takes it to a large stone and smashes the shell open. Each song thrush has its own stone or anvil. By examining the broken pieces of shell round an anvil, birdwatchers can discover which kinds of snail the song thrush likes best.

The blackbird, really a woodland species, is frequently found in gardens. It spends much of its time on the ground searching for food underneath fallen leaves and twigs. As the bird tosses the leaves in all directions, it makes so much rustling noise that it is often mistaken for a small mammal.

garden, where there are hedges, flower beds, fruit trees and vegetable patches, there are more birds, and more different kinds. Common species include the blue tit, great tit, song thrush, magpie, greenfinch, goldfinch, wren and woodpigeon. Very large gardens, with open spaces, wooded areas and bushy thickets, resemble the true countryside. As a result, they attract a wide range of birds. As well as the species already mentioned, there will be others like the mistle thrush, chaffinch, bullfinch, coal tit, long-tailed tit, goldcrest, nuthatch, jay, great spotted woodpecker, green woodpecker, crow and jackdaw.

Although many different birds live in gardens, officially there is no such thing as a 'garden bird'. All the birds found in gardens belong to a natural habitat – for example, hedgerows or woodland – and they only settle in gardens that have similar features. Woodpeckers feed on tree insects and so choose gardens with big, mature trees; while song thrushes look out for hedges and bushes thick enough to hide their nests.

But in spite of their different backgrounds, garden birds do have something in common. They have learnt to live alongside humans and, in many cases, have acquired new habits like feeding on a bird table and using a nest box.

For and against

Gardens have many advantages for birds. Surrounding walls, hedges and fences give protection from

The robin, always alert and perky, is a very familiar garden bird and has become quite tame. It is particularly friendly when flower beds and vegetable plots are being dug: then, the little red-breast keeps close to the gardener, looking out for insects and worms in the fresh-turned earth.

A cock blackbird feeding its young. Blackbirds normally live on insects, worms, snails and berries but in winter often rely on scraps of food left out for them.

The song thrush, 23 cm, found in gardens and woodlands, has a brown back and spotted breast. When singing, it repeats each tune two or three times.

The blackbird, 25 cm, greets dawn and dusk with its clear song. Males are black with a yellow bill; females are brown.

The dunnock, 15 cm, or hedge sparrow has a brown back, grey head and thin beak. It lives low down in hedges and bushes.

cold winds and driving rain. Flowers, shrubs, bushes and trees provide food and nesting sites. And if the garden owners are interested in wildlife there will still be a supply of food and water during the winter on bird tables and in bird baths.

But there are some disadvantages. If birds become dependent on artificial feeding (bird tables, food nets, half-coconuts, peanut strings) they are at risk whenever the people go away: an empty bird table in freezing weather can mean disaster. Then there is danger from killer sprays used to control weeds, insects and plant diseases. Finally, many gardens contain a cat – the traditional enemy of all small birds, especially at breeding time.

Visitors

Not all birds seen in a garden are residents. Some are just passers-by, either migrants flying north-south or travellers on the move from one area to another.

The goldfinch, 12 cm, is a handsome bird with its crimson face and wide yellow wing bar. Its natural habitat is open country with scattered trees and bushes where it feeds on seeds and some insects.

The greenfinch, 14 cm, green-brown with yellow spots on tail and wings, comes from open country. It eats seeds, berries and buds.

The swallow, 19 cm, with blue back, red throat and long forked tail, flies fast and low chasing insects. It often nests inside buildings.

Herons, for example, flying from river to river (or from lake to lake) frequently break their journey at a garden pond for a rest and a quick goldfish snack. Similarly, woodland birds do not like being in the open and, if a journey from one wood to another takes them across an urban area, they use garden trees as 'stepping stones'.

Garden watch

Birdwatchers, particularly beginners, can find plenty to interest them in a garden – all within sight through a window. Many garden birds are so used to people that they become quite tame and do not fly away at the slightest sound or movement. This makes it much easier for observers to recognize common species and to study them as they feed, drink, build nests, warn off intruders, clean themselves and teach their young to fly.

It is even possible to increase the bird life of a garden. Ways of doing this include providing different foods, growing certain seed and berry plants and having a mixture of trees and bushes (see page 102).

A spotted flycatcher, nesting in a gap in a wall. These little birds are found in parks, orchards, gardens and the edges of woods; they nest on buildings and treetrunks, often behind creepers. The young birds are spotted but the adults are streaked instead.

Birds in Parks

A park is an oasis for birds in towns and cities. There they find water to drink, seeds and insects to eat, bushes and trees for shelter, twigs and leaves for nest-building and loose soil for dust baths. The ideal park, from a bird's point of view, has wooded areas with tall trees, thick bushes and dense undergrowth as well as 'wild' zones full of nettles, brambles and waving grasses.

Many of the birds frequently found in parks are woodland species. They include the starling, house sparrow, blackbird, blue tit, great tit, robin, wren, song thrush, mistle thrush, greenfinch, chaffinch, tawny owl, crow and woodpigeon. Occasionally, there are also some green and great spotted woodpeckers, jays, spotted flycatchers and jackdaws. In addition, if the park contains a pond or lake, there will be freshwater species such as moorhens, mute swans and mallards. Many lakes have been stocked with a great variety of waterbirds including vividly coloured ducks and even flamingos. Peacocks, too, may strut through the grounds.

Other unfamiliar species which can be seen in parks include migrants, like whitethroats and peregrines, who use the park as a stop-over on their way north and south.

Some parks contain exotic birds such as peafowls. The male peafowl, or peacock, has a long train of brilliant blue-green feathers that fan out into a magnificent display. Peafowls, found wild from India to Indonesia, have been domesticated for centuries. Once bred for food, they are now kept for ornament.

Right: The mandarin duck, originally from China, is kept as an ornamental bird in many parks and public gardens. The male (right) is brightly coloured but the female bird is drab brown. Over the years some ducks have escaped and there are now mandarins living wild in many places.

Opposite: The mute swan, recognizable by its red-orange beak with black knob, is very common on park lakes. It holds its neck, especially when swimming, in a graceful S-curve.

Farther Afield

Watching birds in streets, gardens and parks is a simple business. When you go out to look for birds farther afield, how many you see will depend much more on how you behave.

One of the first things a birdwatcher must learn is how to observe without being observed. If birds become aware of people watching, they take fright and fly away. There are several ways of making yourself less conspicuous. One way is to wear camouflaging clothes. Others include careful movement, and the use of cover and hides.

Softly, softly

A birdwatcher should move slowly and quietly. Avoid splashing through puddles, treading on dead branches that snap and crackle, and making sudden gestures – like pointing excitedly or raising your binoculars too hurriedly. When you are with a group of birdwatchers, always talk in whispers. If you need to communicate with them from a distance, do not shout or wave your arms about; instead, give a pre-arranged whistle signal.

Keeping low

It is impossible to get near birds without using cover. Cover is anything you can hide behind: a tree-trunk, bush, hedge, rocky outcrop, wall, haystack – even a

Above: Many nature reserves have permanent hides which visiting birdwatchers can use. Although the hidden observer can see ahead very clearly, the observation hole restricts the view upwards so that birds in the air are easily missed.

Left: Hides can be bought ready-made but they are also quite easy to construct. The frame from a camp toilet forms an ideal base; cover this with waterproof material in dull shades of grey, green or brown; then cut observation slits in the sides.

Learn to use cover correctly. A stone wall makes an excellent screen and allows you to creep close to the bird without being seen. But do not then spoil all your efforts by suddenly thrusting your head and binoculars over the top of the wall: such an obvious blot against the sky is enough to frighten any bird away. Instead, keep down behind the wall and move cautiously sideways to look through the gate. In this position, the bird will probably not notice you.

parked car. Always try to approach a bird from behind cover, but above all never walk along the skyline. If the wall or hedge you are using is very low, this may mean creeping along on all fours or even flat on your stomach. When you have reached the nearest point possible and want to observe the bird, cautiously look round the cover – not over it. A head suddenly popping up from behind a rock or bush is very conspicuous, outlined against the sky.

Another fieldcraft secret is to move downwind. If the wind is blowing from the bird towards you, it will carry away any unwanted human noise (but will bring the bird's calls to you more clearly).

Hiding holes

For a really close view of birds – and especially for photographing them – observers use a hide. A hide does just what it says: it conceals the watcher. The most usual type is like a small tent. It has a lightweight frame covered in dull-coloured material with observation holes in the sides. A hide should be just large enough for the observer to sit inside reasonably comfortably on a stool behind a camera/telescope tripod. The stool is very important because standing or kneeling for several hours in one place is very tiring.

Even when a hide is well camouflaged birds may be suspicious, especially if they think there is somebody inside. If possible, put the hide in position several days in advance so that the birds get used to its presence. This is particularly important when you are trying to get near a nest; in this case, move the hide forward slightly each day. It is also a good idea for the observer to go into the hide with someone else and then let that other person leave alone. Birds cannot count: when they see one person come out they believe the hide is empty, so they relax and soon return to their normal activities.

Birdwatchers beside an estuary with binoculars and a telescope. Estuaries are among the most rewarding of all places to visit, especially when they are crowded with migrating birds.

Bird welfare
Birdwatchers do not just look *at* birds, they also look *after* them. Always remember to put the bird's welfare first; its needs are more important than your records and photos. Do not disturb birds unnecessarily, especially during the breeding season. Never track down a bird to its nest if doing so means damaging the surrounding vegetation, as this could expose the nest to enemies.

If a bird is calling anxiously, move away: it may have a nest nearby with eggs or hungry chicks. And if you discover fledglings on the ground, apparently

A group of birdwatchers scanning the beach. Because there is no natural cover along this exposed coast, they are using the sea wall to hide from the birds below.

abandoned, leave them alone; the parent birds are almost certainly close and will come and look after their young as soon as you have gone.

Country care

Birdwatchers spend a lot of time in the country and enjoy being there. So it is only right that they should do their best to look after it. This means respecting all wildlife (not just birds). For example, do not frighten grazing animals, break off living branches, dig up flowers or carve your initials on a tree.

Care of the countryside also means respecting farm life. Remember to shut gates – if cows stray into a field of wheat they can do immense damage; to keep to footpaths – not tramp across farmland or trespass on private ground; to watch over picnic fires, especially in summer when hay, heathland and bracken catch alight so easily; to control dogs (not good birdwatchers, anyway) and stop them from annoying animals and running through crops; and to leave no litter: not only do empty cans and plastic bags look ugly, they can kill small creatures and cause great pain to larger farm animals. In short, make certain that no one has any reason to be sorry that you visited their part of the countryside.

Modern agriculture is driving birds away from farmland. Intensive crop-spraying kills many insects and wild plants, leaving the birds little to feed on. There is also a growing shortage of nesting sites. Hedges are either completely destroyed to make larger fields or are cut back so closely that they are no longer thick enough to conceal nests.

Farmland Birds

Long ago, forests and marshes covered most of Britain. But over the centuries the forests were cut down and the marshes drained to make room for growing crops and raising animals. From a bird's point of view, farmland contains a variety of habitats – fields, hedgerows, scattered trees and isolated buildings.

Fields
Many of the birds found on open farmland are living off the farmer – among them sparrows, skylarks and rooks which invade crop fields to eat vegetables and grains. Gulls follow the plough to seize worms and grubs from the newly turned earth.

Cultivated fields provide an ideal home for mice and short-tailed voles, so two birds which feed on these small animals – the kestrel and the barn owl – are never far away.

After harvest
On open farmland the bird population increases during autumn and winter. When crops have been

From the farmer's point of view, many of the birds that feed in his fields are unwelcome visitors. Woodpigeons are probably the greatest enemy: they eat a variety of young crops and may cost farmers in Britain alone £1 million in a single year. Starlings and rooks attack germinating cereals such as wheat, barley and oats and help themselves to food put out for cattle. Geese and even swans do a considerable amount of damage to growing crops. In orchards, bullfinches destroy thousands of buds on apple, pear, plum and cherry trees.

Tree sparrows are country birds: they feed in fields and nest in tree holes in nearby woodlands. They are closely related to house sparrows, which generally live near people. The two sparrows are very similar. The main difference is in the colour of the crown. The male house sparrow has a grey crown; both sexes of the tree sparrow have a chestnut crown.

Wood pigeons feed on farmland and roost and nest in neighbouring woods. Because of the damage they do to crops they have become one of agriculture's greatest enemies.

harvested, flocks of starlings, jackdaws, rooks, skylarks, house and tree sparrows feed on the stubble fields. Later, they are joined by lapwings, curlews and ducks – principally mallard and teal. In some places geese flock on to farmland during the winter to feed in stubble, potato and carrot fields. In winter, too, pheasants and partridges emerge from the woods, while short-eared owls and hen harriers may come down from moorlands in search of small mammal food.

Many farmland birds protect crops by feeding on harmful insects. Rooks, for example, eat leatherjackets – larvae of the crane-fly, which is a serious crop pest. Rooks are sociable birds: they live in huge flocks and nest in colonies.

Hedges

The bushes and hedges round the edge of a field provide nesting sites for many small birds. At the hedge base the thick undergrowth – a tangled mass of brambles, nettles and grasses – contains plenty of berry, seed and insect food. Whitethroats, for example, love this sort of place and have the country name of 'nettle creeper'. Other common hedgerow birds include finches, dunnocks and warblers – especially blackcaps – yellowhammers and reed buntings. (Reed buntings, really marsh birds, have spread out to colonize overgrown ditches and banks in quite dry places. They are a good example of how a species can adapt to a different environment.)

Trees

Clumps of trees and small woods dot every farm landscape. These tree areas are inhabited by 'woodland edge' birds such as blackbirds, robins, wrens, warblers and tits. Look out, especially, for the long-tailed tit's delicate domed nest.

Farm buildings

Various birds live around farm buildings where there is always a good supply of grain for food and

The wood pigeon, 40 cm, is greyish brown with a rosy breast and a distinctive white patch on the neck and a broad white wing bar. It feeds on open land but at dusk flies into woods to roost.

The rook, 45 cm, is very similar to the crow but has a pale patch round the bill. Found in open country with nearby woods for roosting and nesting, it lives in flocks.

The carrion crow, 45 cm, is black all over with a strong curved beak. It prefers open farmland but needs some trees for nesting. Its varied diet includes small animals, birds' eggs, fruit and berries.

The fieldfare, 25 cm, a grey and brown member of the thrush family, spends the winter in Britain and is often seen in huge flocks scavenging fields for food.

The lapwing, 30 cm, is also called a peewit, after its loud call. Its curved head crest is easy to spot.

The magpie, 44 cm, is black and white with a long tail.

straw for nest construction. Barn-owls and swallows often nest inside barns, while house martins attach their mud nests to the outside. The stores of wheat and other grains attract pigeons, collared doves and house sparrows, while the insect-eating pied wagtail is frequently seen running across the yard.

Danger zones

Many methods now used in agriculture – although they may produce bigger and better crops – are having a very bad effect on wildlife. The trend towards huge fields which involves cutting down hedges and draining marshy areas transforms farmland into a barren, unfriendly place for birds.

Another modern practice which is even more harmful to birds is crop-spraying. The powerful chemicals destroy insects and weeds – both valuable sources of food for birds. As a result some species are in danger of disappearing from farmland habitats. Two examples of birds threatened in this way are the goldfinch and the partridge. Goldfinches flutter alongside hedges feeding on seeds, particularly thistles; but today crop sprays are ruthlessly destroying thistles and so depriving the goldfinch of food. Partridges, on the other hand, rely on insects to feed their young; once again, sprays are killing off the insects and leaving partridges with a survival problem.

Cultivating attracts large flocks of gulls, especially black-headed gulls. They greedily feed on the worms and grubs dug up by the plough as it turns the soil over.

Woodlands and Forests

Today only a few areas remain of the ancient woodland which once covered much of the land. In some places, however, new forests are being planted to supply timber for building, paper-making and other industries, and woodlands hold a marvellous and exciting variety of bird life.

Woodland types

There are two main kinds of woods and forests: coniferous and deciduous. Coniferous forests have trees like pine, fir and spruce. These trees, called conifers, are evergreen: their needle-like leaves do not fall in winter. As a result conifers cast shadow all year long and the ground below them is rather bare.

Deciduous trees include ash, oak, beech and elm. Unlike conifers, they have broad leaves which they shed in autumn. Sunlight can filter through the bare branches to reach the forest floor in early spring, encouraging many flowers to bloom before new leaves appear on the trees. Various bushes also grow

Above: The blackcap, a warbler, lives in bushy undergrowth around the edges of woods and in thick hedges. It eats insects, berries and fruit.

Above: Jays are colourful members of the crow family often seen in oak woodlands. In autumn they collect and bury acorns for use as food during the winter, but frequently forget where the acorns are stored.

Right: The great spotted woodpecker uses its sharp beak to drill a hole in a tree trunk for its nest. It feeds on insects, seeds and berries.

Left: For birds, woodlands should have a layer of thick bushy undergrowth spreading beneath the trees. As these low plants and bushes need sunlight to grow, they only occur where there is a break in the tree canopy. As a result many birds live around woodland edges and clearings.

Right: The chiffchaff, 10 cm, has grey-green plumage which blends with leaves and twigs. It lives in woods, nests near the ground and feeds on insects.

Below: The green woodpecker, 31 cm, has a vivid plumage: bright green back, pale green underparts, a red head and black eye patch.

Left: The bullfinch, 14 cm, has red underparts, a black cap and a stout, strong beak. It feeds on seeds and buds, and lives along woodland edges and in conifer plantations as well as in gardens and parks. The female is much duller.

up. Rather different kinds of birds live in the different types of forest.

Woods for birds

Woodland habitats can contain a marvellous variety of birdlife. From a bird's point of view the ideal wood consists of three layers: a ground layer of low plants and ferns; a shrub layer of bushes and young trees; and the canopy of the trees themselves. Many woodland birds feed on the seeds and fruits of the plants and trees. Others eat the insects and grubs that live either in the undergrowth or on the decaying leaves, rotting branches and fungi of the forest floor.

Coniferous woodlands

In some coniferous forests – native forests – the trees have grown naturally; in others, they have been planted as a commercial crop for timber farming.

Often the 'timber farm' type of forest is an inhospitable place for birds as it contains little in the way of seed or insect food. The conifers grown are mostly foreign species (chosen because they mature quickly); away from their own natural environment they do not attract many insects. The trees themselves are planted so close together that no undergrowth can survive. But while the plantation is still very young, some undergrowth does develop and whinchats and hen harriers may move in for a few

Birches are the first new trees to appear on an area that has been deforested because their light seeds are easily carried on the wind. They are fast-growing and rapidly take over. Birch trees hold a good variety of insect life and several birds, especially redpolls, are attracted by their seeds.

50

Left: The chaffinch, 15 cm, is a very common bird seen in deciduous woods, hedges, parks and gardens. It is easily recognized in flight by its white wing bars and white outer tail feathers. Chaffinches eat seeds and insects.

Right: The wren, 10 cm, is a small brown bird with an amazingly loud song. Wrens live in thick hedgerows and undergrowth where they feed on insects.

Above: The pheasant, 82 cm, is a colourful gamebird found in many areas. Pheasants nest along woodland edges but often feed on open fields.

The goldcrest, only 9 cm long, is the smallest bird in Europe. Its favourite habitat is coniferous forest, where it flutters among the trees searching for insect food. The goldcrest hangs its basket-shaped nest of moss from a branch.

years. Also, the edges of these commercial plantations provide cover for small mammals, particularly short-tailed voles – the staple food of the short-eared owl.

Native coniferous woodlands have a larger and more interesting bird population. Common species found among the pines and firs include redpolls, goldcrests, coal tits and chaffinches. Warblers and woodpeckers may come in for the summer and there are also some birds of prey, especially goshawks and owls. In Britain, the crested tit is seen only in coniferous forests, although elsewhere in Europe it is quite widespread. Two birds that are very much at home among conifers are the crossbill and the capercaillie. Both these birds, found in Scotland and mountainous areas of Europe, can feed from the trees themselves; most other species cannot. The crossbill uses its scissor-shaped beak to tear open pine and fir cones and then eats the seeds inside. The capercaillie, an exotic-looking grouse, feeds on pine needles, shoots and seeds.

Wetlands

When freshwater marshes and other wetlands start drying out – perhaps because of new drainage schemes – willows and alders are among the first trees to grow. They in turn attract birds, especially siskins, which love to feed on alder seeds in winter, and warblers.

The hawfinch spends most of its time among the tree tops of deciduous woodlands. It has a strong, heavy bill for cracking open seeds and fruit stones.

Deciduous woodlands

Deciduous woods and forests provide nesting sites and food for a wide range of birds, especially during the summer. There are all kinds of seed-eaters and fruit-eaters such as finches, thrushes, pigeons and jays and just as many insect-eaters like tits and warblers. Tree-creepers, nuthatches, woodpeckers and other tree-living species are common while birds of prey like sparrowhawks and tawny owls feed on small woodland creatures, including birds. Several birds, such as starlings and crows, roost in woods at night.

Down at ground level game birds, like pheasants and partridges, often breed in the shelter of the woodland edge while the thick undergrowth, all bushes and brambles, makes a good nesting place for wrens and other small birds. In autumn, however, many birds desert the woods and forests. Some are migrants and so fly south to the sun. Others prefer to spend the winter months on open farmland, scavenging the fields for food.

In deciduous woodlands, one kind of tree often predominates: there are, for example, oak woods, beech woods and birch woods – each with its own special birds.

Oak woods

Oak woodlands have a great variety of insect life which makes them an ideal habitat for insect-eating birds. Another advantage is that older oak trees and dead stumps often have holes in them which provide safe nesting places. In fact, many typical 'oak' birds are hole-nesters: the green woodpecker, spotted

Gamebirds get their name because they are mainly hunted for sport. The most common species are partridges and pheasants, both found on farmland and in woodland edges. They are plump birds that live and nest on the ground, rooting for insects and seeds. They seldom fly high or far; when danger threatens, they run away or hide and only take to the air as a very last resort. Game shooting is controlled by law; the birds can only be hunted in autumn and early winter. Many gamebirds are reared on estates solely for shooting purposes.

woodpeckers, pied flycatcher, redstart, nuthatch, tree creeper and various tits. In some areas the buzzard and red kite, both birds of prey, hunt over oak woodlands.

Beech and birch woods

Beech woods have little or no undergrowth. And because there is no real cover, there are very few ground-loving birds. Typical species found in beech forests include wood warblers and, in winter, flocks of chaffinches and bramblings feeding on the fallen nuts (beech mast).

Birches are often the first trees to grow up again in a deforested area. Two birds commonly seen in birch woods are redpolls, which like the seeds, and willow warblers.

Woodland edges

Many species prefer the edges of woods – where there is more light and more plant growth – to the centre. Woodland edge birds include warblers, robins, blackbirds, thrushes and tits.

The pheasant is a familiar gamebird often found along woodland edges. The male's bright colours help it attract a mate while the female's dull brown plumage acts as camouflage, especially at nesting time. Many pheasants are reared by gamekeepers, especially for shooting.

Typical heathlands are covered in bracken or heather and have scattered patches of gorse bushes, birch trees and Scots pines.

Heathlands

Thousands of years ago heathlands did not exist: forests spread everywhere. But Stone Age peoples burnt down many of the trees to make space for growing crops and grazing animals. In places, the land has still not recovered from this harsh fire treatment: these are heathlands.

Heaths, like moors, are wide open areas often covered in heather. But unlike moors they are fairly dry with sandy soils and so have some different plants: bracken, gorse and scattered patches of Scots pines and birch trees.

Today, heaths are in danger of extinction. With the need to use more and more land for agriculture, many heaths have been ploughed up and artificially fertilized. Other heathlands have been planted thickly with conifers. These trees, mostly fast-growing spruces, attract a variety of birds such as redpolls, crossbills, coal tits and goldcrests.

The bird population of a heath varies with the plant life. The linnet, for example, needs some bushes and ground cover; the stonechat likes heather and gorse; the wheatear prefers bare open ground while the nightjar, with its superb camouflage (see page 80), disappears totally among bracken when it settles down during the daytime. It flies at dusk.

The cuckoo normally reaches Britain around the middle of April; its distinctive song is a sure sign that spring has come. During the first weeks after its arrival the male bird chooses a feeding territory and sings his clear, far-carrying 'cuckoo' over and over again to warn off other birds and attract a mate. The female replies with a babbling trill. Later in the season, the male's song turns into a stammering 'cuck . . . cuck'. The traditional rhyme sums this up:

The cuckoo comes in April;
He sings a song in May;
Then in June he changes tune;
In July he flies away.

Linnets are common on open wastelands and heaths, although they need bushes for nesting. In winter they spread over the ground in large flocks searching for seeds.

The whitethroat, a small grey-brown warbler, likes bushy heaths and conifer plantations. It migrates to Africa in winter.

Cuckoos often live in the scattered clumps of trees that dot many heathlands. They feed on insects and grubs and, unlike most birds, will even eat hairy caterpillars.

Birds of prey

Heathlands, especially with close-cropped grass or bare soil, make ideal feeding grounds for birds of prey. Even if the ground cover is thicker and taller – perhaps heather or bracken – a hovering kestrel can easily spot and track down a mouse or vole by the way in which it disturbs the plants as it scuttles along through them.

The kestrel is just as common over heaths as it is over moors, motorways and farmland. It is a member of the falcon family and has a blue-grey head and tail with a dark-spotted, rusty red back. Unlike most birds of prey, which have broad rounded wings, the kestrel's are sharply pointed. It hovers motionless, head down, watching for prey such as fieldmice or beetles, then dives down and pounces on its victim. Kestrels nest high up on rocky ledges or old buildings, or in tall trees where they borrow old nests left by other birds like crows and pigeons.

The hobby, slate-grey with streaky white underparts, is also a falcon. It spends the winter in Africa but although it breeds in many parts of Europe only a few birds – perhaps 300 – come to Britain. They settle in dry heathlands with scattered trees and lay their eggs in the disused nests of other species. Hobbies feed on the wing, catching flying insects and small birds, particularly swallows and martins.

Another bird of prey which likes heathlands – especially the young conifer plantations – is the Montagu's harrier. This bird, grey with a black wing bar, is now very rare in Britain and in some summers none breeds at all. It glides low, searching for small animals, birds, eggs, large insects and even snakes which it plucks from the ground or from vegetation with its rather long, slender legs.

Butcherbirds

Another bird becoming rarer as a breeding species in Britain is the red-backed shrike. This summer visitor was once quite common but now only about a hundred birds come each year. Red-backed shrikes prefer heaths with bushy cover, preferably gorse, thorn and bramble. Red-backed shrikes are like small birds of prey: they speed after victims such as moths, grasshoppers and small birds and seize them with their strong hooked beaks. Like other members of the shrike family, they take prey to their larder – a thorn bush or barbed-wire fence – where they stick it on to a spike; the bird can then tear its food apart more easily. Because of this gruesome habit, shrikes are known as butcherbirds.

Warblers and woodlarks

The only warbler that does not migrate, the Dartford warbler, is a real heathland bird. It is most at home among heather and gorse where it spends the day searching for insects, grubs and spiders. Dartford warblers are small, dark-grey birds with deep-red underparts which build their nests of grass and moss low down under gorse bushes. Because the birds do not migrate they must survive the winter. If the weather is very cold they suffer greatly and so many die that in some years they almost completely disappear.

Another heathland bird that is becoming quite rare is the woodlark. This streaky brown bird prefers land covered in shortish grass with scattered clumps of bushes and trees where it feeds on insects, grubs and, in autumn, on seeds. Like other members of the lark family, the woodlark has a beautiful song; it often flies round in a circle as it sings.

Among the stones

On an open heathland which has dry stony soil and very short grass, you may hear the harsh whistle of the stone curlew. But there is little chance of seeing it: the sandy-brown bird, streaked with black, is so well camouflaged that it blends perfectly with the stony earth. Even when the stone curlew is active it

The skylark makes its nest on the ground, hiding it among the grass. It has a varied diet and will eat seeds and growing shoots as well as insects and worms.

The stonechat, 12 cm, is usually seen perched erect on the top of a bush. The male bird has a black hood and orange-brown breast. Stonechats eat insects.

The cuckoo, 33 cm, is grey with barred underparts. The familiar 'cuckoo' call belongs to the male.

The skylark, 18 cm, is dull brown with a small head-crest. It damages crops by eating the shoots.

is hard to see since it prefers the shadowy hours of dawn and dusk. Once spotted, however, it is easily identified by its large yellow eyes and long, thick yellow legs (its nickname is 'thick-knee'). Stone curlews eat insects, snails and worms and lay their eggs on the bare earth. They are summer visitors but each year fewer birds come to Britain, because their habitat is disappearing into farmland and conifer plantations.

The hobby often breeds in deserted crows' nests. With its long wings it can make high-speed manoeuvres as it chases insects and small birds through the air.

Common birds

Many of the birds seen and heard on heathlands are common species such as cuckoos, linnets, willow warblers and skylarks. The cuckoo, recognized by its two-note call, is notorious for the way in which it lays eggs in other birds' nests so that its young are reared by foster parents. Skylarks are also identified by their song, a strong warble given while they hover high in their air; they are among the first birds to sing at dawn. Willow warblers, small green and yellow birds, like bush heathlands where they feed on insects. Linnets, rosy red in summer, prefer open heaths and eat mostly seeds.

Many birds live on mountains and moorlands during the breeding season. But in winter most of them leave these bleak upland habitats. One common species that does stay throughout the year is the red grouse, a valuable gamebird.

Moors and Mountains

At first sight, moors and mountains seem unfriendly places. They are exposed highlands, cold and windy, with nothing but coarse grass and bare rock. It is difficult to imagine that birds can survive in such habitats. Nevertheless, many species do.

Moorlands

Moors are high, open areas covered with rough grass or other low plants such as heather. They are so dry and windswept that there are very few trees – except for some commercial plantations of conifers.

The most typical bird of heather moors is the red grouse. It lives there all year round, feeding on heather shoots and seeds and on the berries of other upland plants like the bilberry. Grouse are popular

Dotterels are rare in Britain, but occasionally they come in summer to nest on high mountains in Scotland. Unlike most other birds, the female is more colourful than the male and does all the courting. The male bird acts as 'mother' by sitting on the nest, hatching the eggs and then looking after the chicks.

The curlew, a familiar wader, is very much at home on a moorland bog. Curlews and other waders come inland to breed but return to the seashore for winter.

For thousands of years birds of prey have been trained to hunt for men. Among those used for falconry, as this sport is called, are hawks such as the goshawk and sparrowhawk, and falcons including the peregrine and merlin. Falconers protect their carrying hand from the bird's talons with a thick glove, and cover its head with a hood which calms it if it is becoming overexcited.

The hooded crow is very similar to its close relative, the carrion crow. But instead of being black all over, it has a grey back and underparts and is only found in uplands.

gamebirds and in many places their habitat is artificially controlled for shooting purposes.

On some moorlands, stone walls form part of the scenery and are popular with wheatears and stonechats. Both birds nest on the ground, often among stones, and feed on insects.

Spring visitors

The heather landscape is frequently broken by grassy hollows and rocky outcrops. Meadow pipits and twites live in such places during the spring and summer, then move down to warmer valleys and lowlands for winter. Several other species breed on moorlands but desert them in winter. They include many waders such as plovers, sandpipers, curlews, dunlins and greenshanks. These water-loving birds usually settle around bogs and pools and on the stony banks of moorland streams. Such streams sometimes have mountain ash (rowan) trees growing alongside; the bright red rowan berries attract thrushes and ring ouzels in autumn.

Birds of prey

For a long time, birds of prey on moorlands were killed off by gamekeepers in order to protect grouse and other gamebirds. In places, some species were destroyed so effectively that they completely disappeared. But today conservation laws have put an end to the killing and birds of prey are now on the increase. The planting of conifers has also helped their survival since the plantations provide food and cover for their prey.

In spring the male black grouse, or blackcock, courts a female by raising a beautiful fan of white feathers. A group of males will gather on a communal display ground, where for some days they dance and fight in front of the hen birds which are attracted by the gobbling noises.

Three typical birds of prey found on uplands are the hen harrier, merlin and short-eared owl. The hen harrier hunts low over many northern moors: its diet consists of small mammals and large insects. The merlin, a very small, very fast falcon, nests either on the ground among heather or in old crows' nests. Like other falcons, the merlin is a spectacular hunter: it speeds over moorlands, taking the victim bird by surprise and twisting and turning in pursuit of it like a homing missile. It feeds on small birds, particularly meadow pipits. But like its prey, the merlin leaves the moors in winter, moving down to coasts and estuaries. The short-eared owl often hunts by day, flying low like a harrier and looking out for small mammals.

Mountains

Mountain slopes are usually covered with a belt of deciduous forest, then a higher belt of coniferous forest leading to the tree line – the upper limit of tree growth. Above this line there are only low plants and, at the summit, probably nothing but bare rock. But even at such heights, birds make their home. Some, like the ptarmigan, scratch a living from the ground by eating plants or insects. The ptarmigan, which is a mountain relative of the red grouse, breeds

The red grouse, 37 cm, is a familiar gamebird in upland areas; it has a red patch over its eye.

The merlin, 30 cm, is a small, fast falcon, often seen perching on large stones or posts.

The buzzard, 52 cm, is usually a silent bird but can make a piercing mew when it soars.

among boulders and scree above the tree line and even spends winter on the high slopes.

Snow buntings breed in the same nabitats as ptarmigans, although they leave the mountains for coastal lowlands and shores during the bleak winter months. In winter, both the ptarmigan and the snow bunting change their plumage to white which acts as camouflage against the snow.

Overhead, golden eagles soar high, riding the gusts of wind as they seek prey on the ground below. Their chief food is the blue hare but they also eat ptarmigan and red grouse. Another bird of prey, the peregrine falcon, uses mountain crags for nesting; the peregrine is a high-speed killer, swooping down on its victim at 130 km an hour. Buzzards too may nest on rock ledges. Choughs and ravens, both members of the crow family, also fly at great heights, ready to scavenge anything they can find.

Like other birds of prey, the golden eagle has a powerful hooked beak which it uses for tearing prey apart. It also has extremely good eyesight and can spot a rabbit from a distance of two kilometres.

Marshlands

The marshy shores of freshwater lakes and ponds are alive with all kinds of birds. Some breed there; some come for winter; and some are permanent residents, staying all year.

Reed beds
The beds of tall reeds that stretch along the water's edge provide birds with plenty of insect and seed food and give some protection against enemies, including people, and bad weather. Shy birds like water rails, bearded tits, marsh warblers and Savi's warblers as well as the rare bittern and marsh harrier hide among the dense vegetation. Reed warblers build their nests cunningly slung between the tall stems.

Two marsh birds, the bittern and the water rail, have weird calls which are often heard at dusk. The bittern booms like a foghorn and can be heard five kilometres away, while the water rail squeals like a screaming pig.

At the end of the summer, warblers flock into the reed beds to fatten up on insects ready for their long migration flight to Africa. Swallows, too, often roost in reeds before they leave the country. Then, during the winter, flocks of bearded tits or reedlings may be seen in eastern England.

Dry land
Behind the reeds, where the land is drier, there are thickets of alder and willow trees. In autumn these attract siskins and warblers. Farther inland, low-growing willowherbs, sedges and rushes supply plant and seed food for reed buntings, warblers and, in winter, for moorhens.

Water meadows
Water meadows are low-lying fields that are usually dry in summer but flooded in winter; they often stay under water until early spring.

During winter the flooded meadows are crowded with waterfowl; there are also flocks of Bewick's swans that have migrated south from Siberia. When spring comes, and the floods go down, other birds arrive including snipe, redshanks, lapwings, black-headed gulls and, in a few places, the rare black-tailed godwit and ruff.

Above: Reed beds, round the banks of lakes and ponds, are home for many seed-eating and insect-eating birds.

Above: In summer, low-lying meadows are used for grazing cattle and producing hay. But when winter rains flood them with water they become ideal places for waterfowl, particularly dabbling ducks. Next spring, as the floods subside, various waders come to breed.

Opposite: A pair of reed warblers with their nest of leaves and grasses slung between thick reed stems. The cuckoo often chooses a reed warbler's nest as a foster home for its egg. The reed warbler is rarely seen away from marshes; it eats insects and, in autumn, some berries.

Rivers, Canals and Lakes

Birdwatchers always find plenty to see around fresh water. There are birds swimming on the surface, nibbling at aquatic plants, or diving for fish; some are wading in the shallows, some digging in the damp soil along the edge; others are swooping low over the water surface or flying high overhead. But just as rivers and lakes attract birds, they attract humans too. People come to sail, fish, swim, picnic and water-ski; and, if they are not careful, they can harm or even destroy the habitat and its wildlife.

The geography of a river, canal, lake or reservoir affects its bird population. A rushing mountain stream, for example, does not attract the same birds as a sleepy lowland canal.

The grey wagtail – grey back, black wings and yellow underparts – is found near fast-flowing streams. It builds its nest, made of moss and grasses lined with hair, in nooks and crannies by the banks of rivers and under bridges.

Lowland waterways

Lowland rivers wind lazily through fields and meadows, carving out shallow banks as they go. These banks provide a home for kingfishers and sand

In fast-flowing rivers the strong current prevents plants from taking root. Most of the birds that live by mountain streams, like dippers and grey wagtails, feed on insects and tiny water creatures, sometimes catching them under water.

Moorhens use reed leaves to build a platform nest at the water's edge. They feed on plants and tiny creatures which they find on the water surface, along muddy banks and sometimes in waterside fields.

Many waterbirds have webbed feet for strong swimming and flattened legs which offer less resistance to the water. Their feet are often set towards the back of the body – a good position for swimming but one which makes them clumsy on land. Diving birds must be heavy enough to submerge easily, so they have fewer hollow bones and smaller air sacs than totally airborne birds. Grebes even carry stones in their stomachs as extra ballast. Water-birds must keep their bodies dry and warm, so their plumage is extra thick and oily.

In slow-moving or still water, plants are able to take root. Because these plants support all kinds of insect life they make rich feeding grounds for birds. The vegetation also provides safe nesting sites.

martins; both species excavate tunnels into the bank and lay their eggs inside. Sand martins, brown with white underparts, are very sociable. They nest in colonies of up to 200 birds and do everything together: feed, roost and then, in early autumn, fly off to Africa. Sedge warblers and reed buntings live in the bankside vegetation. Pied wagtails usually nest and breed near slow-moving rivers; but outside the breeding season they are found in many places.

Often a meandering river leaves small pools (ox-bow lakes) along its course. This type of pool may be inhabited by a pair of mute swans; they are so aggressive that they will drive away any other breeding water birds.

Canals are popular with several kinds of water-fowl: moorhens, coots, great crested grebes and little grebes. The grebes live entirely on the water, diving frequently for fish; they build nests of aquatic weeds and anchor them to reeds to stop them floating away. Coots and moorhens eat mostly plants; the coot dives for its food, while the moorhen pecks at surface vegetation. The moorhen is quickly identified by the way it bobs its head and jerks its white tail.

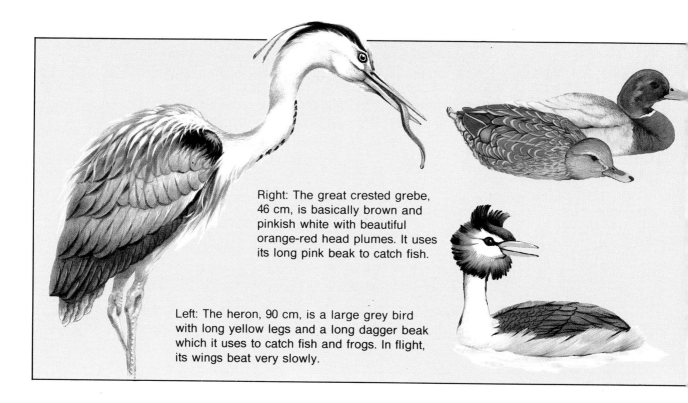

Right: The great crested grebe, 46 cm, is basically brown and pinkish white with beautiful orange-red head plumes. It uses its long pink beak to catch fish.

Left: The heron, 90 cm, is a large grey bird with long yellow legs and a long dagger beak which it uses to catch fish and frogs. In flight, its wings beat very slowly.

Upland rivers

Upland rivers are fast flowing and rush down from moorlands or mountains. The birds of such rivers are adapted to feeding along the stony banks and in tiny pools as well as on the swiftly moving rivers themselves. The best example is the dipper. This small, dark-brown bird perches on rocks midstream to seize small creatures from the surface, and even wades into the water to pick them off the bottom. It nests in the river bank or under a bridge. Grey wagtails also live near fast-flowing water, running rapidly along the water's edge snapping up insects.

Upland lakes

The water in upland lakes often drains off poor, acid soil and so cannot support much insect or plant life. This makes them unattractive to birds except for a few fish-eating species like the goosander. Goosanders live mostly on trout which they catch by diving from the surface; they have thin serrated bills for grasping their prey.

During the winter months, however, upland lakes provide useful roosting sites for large numbers of gulls and some geese which feed away from the lake itself in the countryside around.

Some conservationists feel that these upland lakes should be developed for recreation – sailing, water-skiing, canoeing – so that lowland lakes could be preserved for wildlife.

Swans are the largest birds found in Britain. The most common species, the mute swan, lives here all year; two others, the whooper swan and Bewick's swan, are winter visitors. Once they mate the cob (male) and pen (female) stay together for life. Both partners share in building the nest, incubating the eggs and looking after the young, called cygnets. The swan family keeps together for about nine months, until the beginning of the next breeding season.

Left: The mallard, 58 cm, is the most common duck in Britain. It is found on all kinds of fresh water – rivers, marshes, park lakes, village ponds and even in city fountains!

Left: The coot, 38 cm, is all black except for its white beak and frontal shield. It dives for underwater plant food but also grazes along the banks. To get up into the air, coots have to make a long take-off run along the water.

The mute swan, 150 cm, is the largest British bird. It is all white but for an orange-red beak with black knob; the neck forms a graceful S-shape.

The moorhen, 33 cm, is very common on lakes and rivers. It is black with a white side line and tail feathers; the yellow beak has a red base.

The kingfisher has a large head, small tail and a brilliant plumage, with blue and green upperparts, orange-red underparts. It sits motionless on a waterside branch or post watching the movement of small fish below; then it plunges headlong into the water to catch a fish with its long, spear-like bill.

Lowland lakes

Lowland lakes are usually surrounded by fertile soils, and so the water that drains into them is rich in the minerals and other chemical substances that plants need. There are plants everywhere: underwater, on the surface, along the shores, lining the banks. This vegetation supports a huge insect population, and between them the plants and insects attract many bird species.

Divers and dabblers

Water birds feed in two ways: they either dive underwater or dabble on the surface. A few diving birds feed on fish; among them are grebes, divers (the red-throated diver, found in Scotland, is the most common) and kingfishers. The kingfisher dives from a perch while grebes and divers plunge from the surface. Other birds, like coots and tufted ducks, dive down to feed on underwater plants, insects or tiny creatures on the lake bottom.

Many water birds, such as mallards, shovelers and teals are surface-feeders. They swim around in shallow water, eating floating vegetation, nibbling at shore plants and up-ending to reach roots and shoots below the surface. Mute swans feed in this way and, with their long necks, can feed in deeper water than small ducks.

The dipper, a small dark-brown bird with a vivid white chin and breast, is never far from fast-flowing water. It happily perches on rocks, walks along the stream bed and even swims in its search for food. It eats mostly insect grubs, especially dragonfly nymphs. To help it live in its watery habitat is has special glands producing oil with which to keep its feathers waterproof.

The male mallard is a colourful bird with its green head, white collar, chestnut breast and blue wing patch. The female is all brown except for the blue wing patch. Mallards nest on the ground, hidden by a bush, tall grass or an old wall, but never far from water. Only the female makes the familiar 'quack quack' call.

A pair of mute swans by their nest at the water's edge. The nest is built of reeds, leaves and grasses and is added to each breeding season; normally, swans use the same nest year after year. They mate for life and look after their young, called cygnets, until the start of the next breeding season. This swan is called 'mute' because it does not have a distinct call like other swans; but it does have a fierce hiss. Mute swans are very aggressive birds and will drive off all intruders.

The red-necked grebe breeds in northern lands and only spends winter in Britain. In summer this grebe has a chestnut-red neck and brownish back, but in winter its plumage becomes grey. Like other grebes, it dives for fish and aquatic insects.

Herons

One of the most distinctive freshwater birds is the heron, which lives by lakes, reservoirs and marshes. This large bird is mainly grey, but has a white neck and head with a black crest. The heron eats fish and can often be seen standing motionless in the water, waiting for a fish to swim within reach of its dagger-like beak. It also catches frogs and other small animals.

Winter visitors

As migration time approaches, large numbers of swallows, martins and swifts gather over lakes to fatten up on insects before their long flight. Many freshwater birds, among them the grebes and divers, move to the seashore for winter, but their place on the lake is taken by flocks of roosting gulls.

Estuaries

An estuary, flat and open and washed by tides, offers no shelter for nesting birds. But in winter it provides feeding and roosting sites for thousands of migrants, especially waders. Some come just a short way from inland marshes and moors; others are long-distance travellers from breeding grounds in the Arctic. Birdwatching in estuaries is particularly exciting at migration time when unusual birds may visit to feed on their way north or south.

Time by the tide

The lives of estuary birds are governed more by tides than by daylight hours. They feed at low tide when the mudflats are exposed and then roost while their feeding areas are covered by water.

Mudwatch

The best way of seeing the birds that inhabit estuaries is to find out where they roost at high tide. Then, choose a hiding-place near the roost and watch as the incoming tide pushes the birds landwards on to remaining areas of mud.

The birdwatcher will soon discover how each species prefers a certain part of the estuary – the part where it can find its favourite food. For example, although waders appear similar to one another, with their long legs and slender bills, they have different diets. Some like the mini-shrimps and cockles found on the mud surface; others prefer worms; some choose tiny creatures buried in the mud; some favour fish; others eat vegetation. By watching how each species feeds, picking at the surface or probing into the mud, it is possible to understand how so many birds can live together without too much competition. And it is especially interesting to notice how the birds' bills are adapted to the way in which they feed; the curlew has a long bill and probes deep into the mud, while the plovers have short bills and feed on worms, grubs and shellfish near the surface.

Other estuary visitors

As well as waders, water birds such as divers, grebes and ducks gather at these rich feeding grounds in winter. At high tide they are scattered over the water surface, but when the tide is low they collect in the

Dowitchers are North American waders which migrate to western Europe in winter, occasionally visiting Britain. They have exceptionally long bills which they use to reach worms and other creatures living in deep mud.

The grey plover breeds in the Arctic tundra, but migrates in winter to estuaries and muddy shores throughout Europe. Like most waders, it has a distinctive and long-reaching mellow whistling call; calls are important for identifying waders.

Oystercatchers in flight over shallow estuary waters. As the tide goes down they gather in large flocks to feed on the shellfish left lying on the mud. The oystercatcher's bill is specially shaped to prise open mussels and other molluscs.

The curlew, 54 cm, has a long curved bill for finding worms in the mud.

The oystercatcher, 42 cm, is black above and white below with a white wing bar and orange beak.

water channels winding across the mud, and are then easier to observe.

Upper estuaries

Higher up estuaries, where salt water begins to give way to fresh water, other species of bird may be found. Outside the breeding season, kingfishers and common sandpipers, for instance, feed in the streams running off the land into the edges of mudflats.

The sides of the upper estuary may be bordered by rough grasslands called saltmarshes – areas where the mudflats are beginning to dry out. In winter, saltmarshes provide undisturbed grazing grounds for huge flocks of migrant geese. Many thousands of barnacle geese, Brent geese, white-fronted geese and pink-footed geese journey south from Greenland to the safety of Britain's milder climate.

Saltmarshes are also visited by merlins, small falcons. During the winter months, these birds of prey forsake their high moorland homes and move down to marshy coasts where they live by hunting waders and other small creatures. The wader population is also in danger from the peregrine – another, larger falcon – which often lives in neighbouring sea cliffs.

During the spring and summer, a few waders – lapwings and redshanks, for example – breed on the saltmarshes, but most species return inland.

Sea Coasts

Sea coasts, with their cliffs, caves, beaches, bays and islands, provide feeding grounds and nesting sites for a variety of birds. Although these seabirds range from the tiny storm petrel (no bigger than a sparrow) to the huge gannet, they have several features in common: an extra large oil gland for keeping feathers waterproof; webbed feet for swimming; a strong beak for catching fish; and, in many cases, a dark back and light underparts for camouflage: seen from above they blend with the waves but from below they merge into the sky.

Like many other wildlife habitats, coasts and oceans are at risk from people and their destructive ways. On the beach, crowds of holiday-makers drive away the birds, especially at breeding time. Out at sea, oil pollution kills many more: as birds swim into an oil slick their feathers clog; their lungs burn and they quickly die.

Life on the ocean waves
Some seabirds live far out in the Atlantic Ocean but even they have to come ashore once a year to breed. These deep-sea species include shearwaters, petrels, the gannet, the kittiwake (a gull) and members of the auk family such as razorbills, guillemots and puffins.

These seafarers have various fishing methods. The

Sea coasts are full of interest but they can also be dangerous and birdwatchers should take extra care. Check out the times of tides; this is particularly important for mudflats and marshes that are submerged at high water. Move cautiously over rocks and across screes and remember that seaweed and spiky grass are often slippery. Above all, keep away from cliff edges and do not attempt to climb up or down cliff faces: they can be loose, crumbling and very treacherous. Lastly, when birdwatching from a boat do wear a lifejacket: if all your attention is focused on a kittiwake's nest you will not notice the freak wave or sudden gust of wind that might throw you overboard.

The puffin, black above and white below, has distinctive white cheeks and a parrot-shaped bill, highly coloured in summer. It flies low over the sea with quick wing beats and when swimming sits high in the water. It feeds on fish which it catches by plunge-diving from the surface. Puffins breed in colonies, usually on the grassy cliff tops of isolated islands. The nest, an unlined burrow, is either built by the birds themselves or borrowed from rabbits; sometimes puffins and rabbits even share the same entrance.

Breeding guillemots crowd on to the top of a rock stack. As guillemots do not build nests there is always the risk of eggs rolling off into the sea. Some kittiwakes are nesting farther down the rock and even lower, on the left, is a cormorant. These big black birds prefer rocky coasts.

auk family, for instance, plunge-dive from the surface and, driven by their wings, can reach 90 metres deep. Gannets dive from high in the air and swallow the fish whole on surfacing.

Inshore birds
Most seabirds, however, stay in coastal waters, and gulls (except for the kittiwake) always keep within sight of land. Gulls are found along the coast

A small rocky islet is an ideal breeding site for many different seabirds. There are no animals to prey on them and, because the rock is difficult to reach and impossible to climb, the birds are also safe from people. Nesting colonies can, and do, make use of every ledge and crevice.

throughout the year, although many go inland for the winter. Cormorants and shags may also be seen at any time of the year, either flying low over the sea or perched on a rock with their wings spread out to dry: their feathers are not very waterproof and become sodden during dives for fish. In winter, eider ducks and mergansers can be seen diving for food near the shore.

In summer the bird population along a coast increases when ocean birds return to breed. This is a good time for birdwatching, as all kinds of species can be spotted flying over the waves seeking food for their young. Terns, which nest in colonies on beaches, can be seen in many places diving from the air into the water in search of food.

Below: Colonies of breeding shags and kittiwakes share this rocky island.

At home on a cliff
Seabirds generally breed in colonies – often on offshore islands or high cliffs where they are safe from disturbance. Petrels, shearwaters and puffins nest in burrows on isolated, grass-topped islands; it is quite common for them to take over rabbit burrows. High, narrow cliff ledges are used as nesting sites by guillemots, razorbills, fulmars and kittiwakes; cormorants and shags on the other hand prefer wider ledges or even caves.

Cliff colonies can become very overcrowded and some birds, especially kittiwakes and fulmars, regularly use the ledges of nearby buildings instead. Terns simply nest on sandy or stony beaches, laying their eggs in a shallow scrape.

The herring gull, 56 cm, is grey and white with black wing tips.

The puffin, 30 cm, is easily identified by its white cheeks and large bill.

The gannet, 90 cm, is a large white bird with black wing tips. Its long wings beat stiffly. Gannets, in huge colonies, build seaweed nests on cliff ledges.

A herring gull with its chick. Gulls build their nests – rough mounds of plant material – on rocky ledges or on the ground. Although the birds nest in colonies, they are not friendly towards one another: if a young bird strays away from its parents it may be attacked and killed by the neighbouring gulls.

Shags, large black birds closely related to cormorants, build untidy nests of seaweed hidden in a cave or behind a boulder. They breed in vast colonies along rocky coasts.

The kittiwake, a grey and white gull with yellow bill and black legs, spends most of its life far out at sea. It comes to land to breed in noisy colonies on steep sea cliffs. Unlike most gulls, kittiwakes build quite a strong nest; they usually have two chicks. Kittiwakes are rather like the common gull and (though much smaller) the herring gull, but have no white markings on their wing tips.

Below: The common tern, a long-winged, grey-white seabird with a black cap, breeds on the ground on lonely beaches and islands. In some areas, terns breed in inland gravel pits in coastal swamps and by lakes because the beaches are full of holidaymakers. Terns feed by flying or hovering just above the waves and snatching food from the surface.

In many cases seabirds lay only one egg. The gannet incubates its egg under its webbed feet – not by sitting on it. Guillemots and razorbills do not build nests; instead, they lay their eggs on the bare rock of the cliff ledge. The eggs themselves are pear-shaped, which means that they are less likely to roll off the edge into the sea.

The name seagull is misleading. The gulls most frequently found in Britain – the black-headed gull, herring gull and common gull – are as much at home inland as along the coast. In fact, some of them have probably never even seen the sea. These have become town birds, picking scraps off rubbish heaps and nesting in buildings; or they live in the country, feeding off farmland and breeding by marshy lakes. But many gulls have two homes: they migrate inland for the winter months then return to coastal dunes and cliffs in spring.

Outsiders

It is not only true seabirds that inhabit coastlines. Some birds that normally nest on inland cliffs will also use sea cliffs; among them are jackdaws, crows, stock doves and kestrels. Rock pipits and rock doves are found along many coasts, and occasionally ravens and buzzards also breed in coastal areas. In some places house sparrows, swifts and even swallows will breed in sea cliffs, while sandy cliffs make ideal places for sand martins to excavate their nest holes. The green woodpecker, too, can be a coast bird: it will nest in rock crevices and feed on colonies of ants along the cliff top. With real luck, a birdwatcher might even see a peregrine falcon or a party of choughs.

These land birds do not get their food from the sea but from the shore and neighbouring countryside. Many work their way along the strand-line, turning over seaweed to look for bits of food.

In autumn and spring a variety of small migrant birds can be found resting in bushes and marshes behind the shore. The seaside is one of the best places to spot migrating birds since many species always follow the coastline for as much of their journey as is possible: land means safety and food and helps to keep them on course.

The fulmar, a grey petrel, roams the oceans and will often follow ships for days scavenging food scraps. When an enemy approaches, the fulmar shoots out a jet of foul-smelling oil from its mouth.

Rare Birds

Some birds are rare from natural causes; others from artificial ones. But whatever the background, spotting a rare bird – especially outside a nature reserve – is a prize experience for any birdwatcher.

Unexpected visitors

Many of Britain's rare birds are just occasional visitors. Some are passing migrants, blown off course. Some are driven here because of food shortages. The snowy owl lives near the Arctic where it feeds on lemmings, but every few years the lemming supply runs out. The snowy owls then move south and one or two have even reached the Shetlands and bred there, though at present only females are living there.

Human enemies

Many birds have become rare, even extinct, because of people: we destroy their habitats, hunt them and pollute their world.

In the 1960s, many peregrine falcons died through eating poisoned prey. Farmers were using the poison to kill pigeons and other pests. But now, with the worst poisons banned, peregrines are increasing in number.

The red kite, 60 cm, feeds on rabbits and other small mammals. By 1900, after years of slaughter, only 12 birds were left in Britain. Today, there are about 70. Toy kites are named after the bird's V-shaped tail.

The bittern, 75 cm, lives in large reed beds where it eats fish, frogs and water insects. In the 1800s, it died out in Britain because of marsh drainage and shooting. But bitterns have come back and now total about 100.

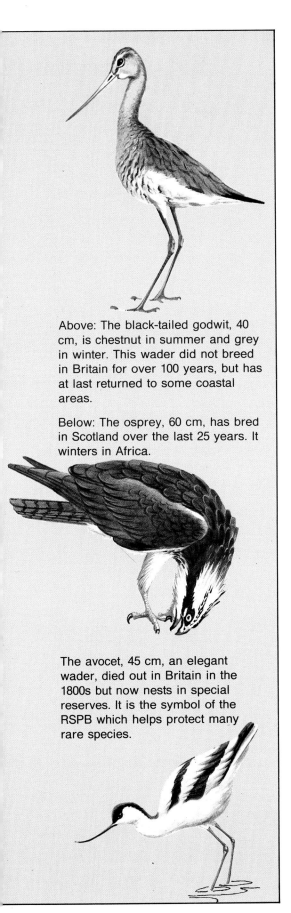

Above: The black-tailed godwit, 40 cm, is chestnut in summer and grey in winter. This wader did not breed in Britain for over 100 years, but has at last returned to some coastal areas.

Below: The osprey, 60 cm, has bred in Scotland over the last 25 years. It winters in Africa.

The avocet, 45 cm, an elegant wader, died out in Britain in the 1800s but now nests in special reserves. It is the symbol of the RSPB which helps protect many rare species.

The osprey, a rare bird of prey, catches its fish food by plunging feet-first into the water.

When a habitat is destroyed, its bird population has nowhere to live. One species which suffered in this way was the avocet, a wader which became extinct in the 1800s following widespread marsh drainage. Recently, it has been successfully nesting again in some bird reserves. Another bird which is making a come-back is the red kite. Once this bird of prey was not uncommon, soaring over hills and scavenging in towns, but gamekeepers nearly hunted it to extinction.

Somewhere safe

Many rare birds are only found in nature reserves. There, they live and breed in natural habitats but are safe from egg-thieves and vandals. Often reserves provide permanent hides for observers to study the birds without disturbing them.

Night Birds

Most birds are day creatures. All their activities – feeding, mating and nest-building – happen between dawn and dusk. At night they are unable to find food so they sleep, protected by the darkness. But there are exceptions: a few birds work at night and rest during the day.

The most famous night birds are owls. When the rest of the world is asleep, owls are on the wing hunting small creatures like mice and voles. Owls are able to hunt in the dark as their very keen eyesight and hearing make them aware of the dimmest shape and slightest noise. Their flight is virtually silent, helping them to pick up the sounds of their prey and to approach without warning.

Waders, because they follow the tides, are often night-feeders, too. They can only probe mudflats for food at low tide – whether in daylight or darkness. Some insect-eaters feed at night. Nightjars, for example, emerge at dusk and hunt into the night: they probably find insects by picking up their flight vibrations. Swifts, on the wing for 24 hours a day, also feed at night.

There are also night-singers such as the nightingale and even the cuckoo. It is possible that birds sing at night because their song carries better in the stillness and is more likely to reach a mate. In towns, robins, dunnocks and blackbirds sometimes sing at night if bright street lights make them think it is day.

Many migrating birds travel by night as well as by day – to get the journey over more quickly!

Opposite: A barn owl carries a shrew to its nest after a successful hunting trip. Large eyes and keen hearing help owls to hunt at night; the soft edges of their wings allow them to fly very quietly, and they can pick up the smallest sounds from the ground. The barn owl's call is a long screech. As its name suggests, it often nests in barns and other old buildings. It seems almost white if caught in the headlights of a car.

The nightjar sleeps during the day, hidden on the ground among dead leaves and twigs, then emerges at night to hunt for insects, especially moths. Its plumage pattern in browns, greys and creams forms one of the best camouflages in the bird world.

Birds and their Bodies

A great deal of information about birds has been collected through ringing. The rings on large birds, like mute swans, are big enough to identify (by colour and letter) without having to recapture the bird.

People have been fascinated by birds for thousands of years. They played a part in several early religions and the sacred ibis was worshipped in ancient Egypt. This is not surprising, for birds are among the most colourful and adaptable of animals. They are comparatively easy creatures to study, and their relationships with one another and with other animals are fascinating. They have complicated patterns of behaviour connected with their breeding and nesting habits, and their bodies' shapes and workings have been intriguingly adapted to flight. Perhaps the most interesting of all is their mysterious migration. Although we know much about their routes we still do not really know how they navigate; and this is the great gap in our knowledge of birds.

Ornithologists – as people who study birds are called – discover a lot about birds by ringing them. The birds are caught for ringing with nets and traps, operated by specially trained ringers. Ringed birds have provided valuable information about population densities, wintering grounds, breeding sites, migration route and life spans.

A turnstone is ringed for a migration study. If it is later found, the number on the ring will help to trace the bird's route. Ringing programmes have taught us a great deal about birds' migration routes, but just how they navigate remains one of the most fascinating mysteries of animal behaviour.

Starlings gather in huge flocks – often thousands of birds together. They roost in buildings, trees and reeds. Sometimes, the flock is so large that the birds completely flatten a reed bed.

Humans have found many uses for birds' feathers and some species have been ruthlessly hunted for them. They have been used to decorate ceremonial clothes and hats; as pens (quills); for arrows and shuttlecocks; and as stuffing for cushions and quilts. Today feathers are less used for decoration, and man-made materials have replaced them for many other things. Those used as stuffing are mostly obtained as by-products of poultry farming.

Netting birds in order to ring them is done by specially trained ringers. Here a rocket net was fired over the gulls while they were feeding.

It is known, for instance, that some species come back each year to the same nest site, and spend the winter at another particular location several thousand kilometres away. Other species breed in one country, migrate, then return to breed somewhere quite different. Probably, while in their winter quarters, they become mixed up with a flock of the same species from another country.

Life span

Most birds die before they are a month old. It is when fledglings first leave the nest that they are most at risk from vandals, cats, weasels, falcons and so on. Even if they survive this perilous period, life is always full of dangers. Some are natural, like droughts or severe frosts; others are artificial like overhead power cables and smog. Many birds die while migrating. If it is lucky, a small bird may live for five or six years, but most die far earlier.

Small birds make up for their short lives by having two or three broods a year, so that in spite of all dangers, one or two young from each pair will grow up.

Larger birds have fewer enemies and so live longer. They do not need to lay so many eggs as smaller birds, and have only one brood a year. Often they may not start to breed until they are five or six years old. Some waders and gulls have been known to reach 30 years old, although 15 years would be about average.

Bone and muscles

Although a bird may look very different from other vertebrates (animals with backbones), it has the same basic structure: a strong skeleton of bones enclosing and protecting the vital organs.

A bird's skeleton is a framework for flying. As birds must stay as light as possible, many of the bones are hollow. The breastbone in front of the ribs is huge, often larger than the rib cage itself. This is because it forms the anchorage for the powerful flight muscles. The wing feathers are attached to long arm and hand bones. To help the bird balance, the leg bones are positioned quite strangely: the thigh and knee are hidden under the plumage and the first visible bone is, in fact, the shin.

In the skull, the jawbones are long and slender and are covered with the horny plates which form the bird's beak or bill. There are no teeth. The skull itself is joined to the rest of the skeleton by a long, flexible neck containing a great many neck bones. A swan has 25 neck bones and a sparrow, 16. (In contrast, mammals – even giraffes – have only seven.) As a result a bird can bend its neck and turn its head easily, which helps it reach food, spot enemies and preen its feathers.

For flying, a bird needs very powerful muscles. The most important are the large wing muscles which are anchored to the breast bone. A bird has strong leg muscles, too, so that it can run, hop and perch; these muscles also cushion the bird when landing.

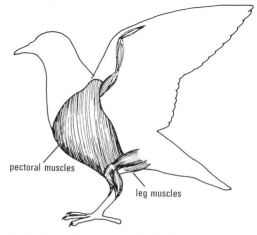

A bird has large, powerful wing muscles to help it fly, and strong leg muscles which cushion the bird when it lands and help it when running or hopping or swimming. Over half a bird's weight is in its muscles.

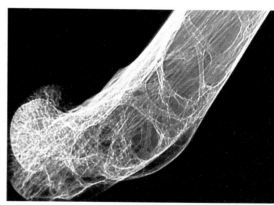

This X-ray of a bone from a pelican shows the many air passages which run through it. Hollow bones help reduce the bird's weight, and so do air sacs inside the body. Birds also digest their food and drop their wastes quickly to stay as light as possible.

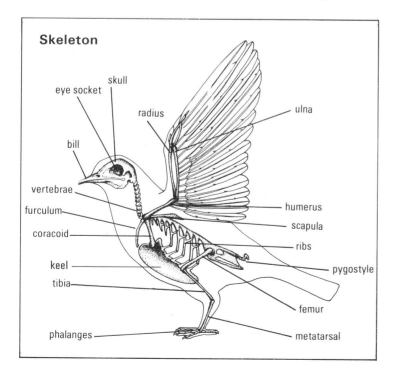

Skeleton

skull
eye socket
radius
ulna
bill
vertebrae
humerus
furculum
scapula
coracoid
ribs
keel
pygostyle
tibia
femur
phalanges
metatarsal

A diagram of a bird's skeleton. Note the long flexible neck, the huge breast bone and the strange position of the leg bone.

Right: Water birds have such thick layers of feathers that they can swim in freezing conditions. The feathers are oily which makes them waterproof. They also conserve body heat and provide protection against the wind. They must be long-lasting, since most birds moult only once or twice a year.

Below: A contour feather. The inset shows how the barbules – tiny hooks – join the barbs together. The central shaft or quill is hollow.

Below right: The wing feather of a bird. The outermost feathers, called the primaries, are attached to the bone that corresponds to the human hand. Feathers attached to the 'arm' are called secondaries. Primaries and secondaries are flight feathers. The feathers covering the bases of the flight feathers are called coverts.

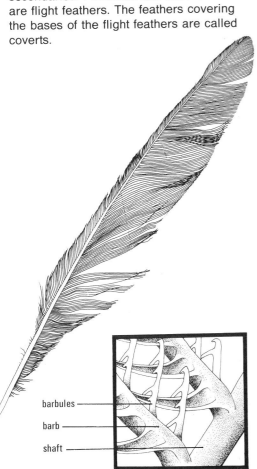

barbules

barb

shaft

Feathers

Birds are the only animals on earth that have feathers. A small bird, like a sparrow, has about 2000 feathers while a swan has as many as 25,000.

Feathers, made of a dead substance called keratin, consist of a central shaft or quill with numerous barbs either side forming the vane; barbules – tiny hooks – link the barbs.

There are two main types of feather: contour and down. Contour feathers cover the body, wings and tail. They are strong and tough, but very light. The body feathers protect the bird from damage while the wing and tail feathers produce and control flight. Down feathers, soft and fluffy, lie beneath the contours to form a warm insulating layer.

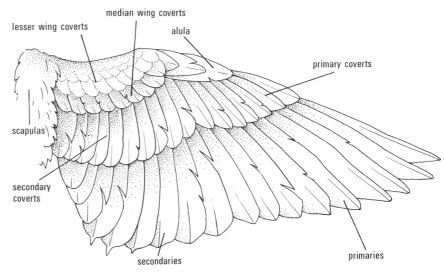

lesser wing coverts

median wing coverts

alula

primary coverts

scapulas

secondary coverts

secondaries

primaries

To clean feathers that are out of reach of its bill, a bird uses its claw like a comb; it scratches out dirt and parasites such as mites and ticks.

House sparrows in the shallow water at the edge of a pond. When land birds bathe, they dip their heads and necks and use their wings to splash water over their backs. Bathing is usually followed by preening.

Feather care

Feathers are vitally important and must be kept in first-class condition. Birds do this in several ways.

The most common method of feather care is preening. The bird runs its beak along each feather: this cleans off dirt and pests, puts the barbules back in place and smooths the vane. With its flexible neck, a bird can reach its back, wings and tail, but not its head. So, to clean its head a bird scratches it with one foot while balancing on the other.

Birds are often seen bathing as well as preening. For water birds, bathing just means diving and rubbing their feathers together under water. Land birds generally splash around in a shallow pool while kingfishers and swallows take a quick dip as they fly low over water. Pigeons and starlings prefer a shower rather than a bath: when it rains, they spread their wings out. If there is fine, dry soil around, sparrows will take a dust bath. Some birds even sit on ants' nests and allow the ants to run through their feathers. Dust and ants may help to remove parasites.

Another important part of feather care is oiling. Birds smear their feathers with a waxy substance obtained from an oil gland near the tail; in water birds this gland is extra large. The substance waterproofs the feathers and may also provide the bird with vitamins.

A bird relies on its feathers for flight, warmth and body protection. It therefore takes great care of them and, like this kingfisher, will preen them thoroughly.

A shelduck moulting. When ducks moult, they lose all their flight feathers at once and so remain flightless until the new feathers have grown. Shelduck from all over northern Europe gather to moult in midsummer in the Heligoland Bight region of north Germany.

Moulting

Feathers do not last forever. As the bird goes about its daily life, they become worn and damaged. Since feathers are made of a dead material, they cannot repair themselves: the only way of renewing the plumage is to replace it. The process of shedding old feathers and growing new ones in their place is called moulting.

Moulting normally happens once a year at the end of the breeding season. Most birds moult gradually, losing only a few feathers at a time: this ensures they can always fly and prevents them from catching cold. The moult usually begins in the wings, then spreads to the body and tail. Various water birds, including ducks, geese and swans, lose all their flight feathers at once and are unable to fly for a short period. During this time they are very shy and keep out of sight – and danger.

Many birds, especially males, have a second moult. This moult is not to replace worn feathers but to brighten up their plumage for the breeding season. A great many birds spend the winter in a dark uniform of grey or brown but put on a more colourful plumage in the spring. Often this plumage change is part of courtship as brighter colours help the male bird to attract a mate. The male chaffinch, for example, replaces its brown crown with a striking blue-grey one.

From take-off to touch down. As well as noting wing positions, watch how the bird holds its tail and feet.

For take-off, the wings are lifted, then brought down with a strong thrusting action against the sides of the body.

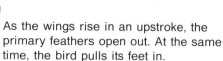

As the wings rise in an upstroke, the primary feathers open out. At the same time, the bird pulls its feet in.

This blue tit, coming in to land, brakes by spreading its wings and tail; it then brings the wings back to the folded position. Take-off and landing need practice when birds are learning to fly and their antics are sometimes very comic to watch.

Flight

Nearly all birds are skilled fliers, and some, like the swifts, spend almost completely air-borne lives. Birds fly by 'swimming' through the air, using air currents for lift and controlling the flow of air through their primary feathers. A bird's wing is slightly curved on top; this means that air passing over it has to move farther and so faster than air under the wing. As a result, the wing is pushed upward. Lift is also produced by making the air move downwards; a bird does this when it flaps its wings.

Once it is up in the air, a bird moves itself forward by pushing the air back and away with its wings. As the wing comes down, the primary feathers close to

On landing, the wings return to the folded position; legs and feet cushion the impact.

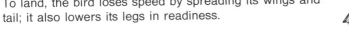

To land, the bird loses speed by spreading its wings and tail; it also lowers its legs in readiness.

push strongly against the air. On the upstroke, the primaries spread out, allowing the air to pass through freely. The bird uses its tail as a rudder and, for turning, can also tilt its wings and body.

Some birds are able to hover: they flap their wings in such a way that they produce lift but no forward motion. Others, like kestrels, hover by flying into the wind at the same speed as the wind itself is blowing; this makes them stay in the same spot.

Some birds – especially seabirds and birds of prey – use warm air currents to help them soar and glide with little effort. They soar upwards on the warm current to a great height, and at the current's peak they peel off and glide, gradually losing height, until they hit the next warm current. This soaring and gliding flight is particularly useful for birds on migration, as it allows them to travel long distances without using too much energy. But these warm currents rise only in the day, and from land.

Below left: A heron about to land. When flying, birds tuck their feet up out of the way or, in the case of long-legged species, they let them trail behind. Just before landing, the feet are dropped – like a plane's undercarriage – ready to grasp a perch or settle on the ground.

Below: A gannet makes use of an up-current of air which allows it to hang effortlessly over the seashore.

Feeding and digestion

Each habitat can support a number of different kinds of birds, provided that they are species that do not compete with one another. Each species has its own needs in food, its own ways of feeding. Under the cover of bushes and trees, several kinds of insect eaters may search for food, each choosing its special area between the ground scrub layer and the upper canopy of the largest trees. Even in your garden, you can soon see how birds favour a particular feeding ground. Dunnocks forage on the ground under cover of bushes, wrens creep along the bases of walls, peering into nooks and crannies, and warblers explore higher up in the bushes, looking for insects among the leaves. On a lake, each kind of waterfowl will choose a particular area depending on the depth of the water and food available there.

Birds have no teeth, although fish-eaters may have serrated edges on their beaks for holding prey. Some birds swallow their food whole; some, like finches with seeds, break it up inside their bills; while others, like hawks, hold it with their feet and tear off bits to swallow. A few birds even use tools to help them get at their food: song thrushes smash snail shells against a big stone while gulls break open crabs and shellfish by dropping them on to rocks. Many seed-eaters swallow grit and store it in a special part of the digestive system known as the gizzard. Strong muscles in the gizzard churn round the seeds, which become ground up by the grit.

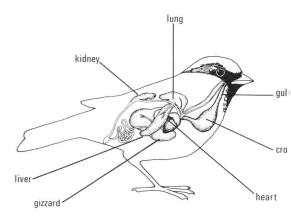

Food is swallowed into the crop, where some may be kept for passing on to the chicks. Many birds have a gizzard, a muscular part of the stomach containing small stones it has swallowed to help crush its food. Birds of prey have no gizzard but special gland to help break down raw meat or fish. Solid and fluid waste are excreted through the cloaca.

Above: A pellet from an eagle owl. Most birds of prey produce long, cylinder-shaped pellets; some seabirds have round ones. Pellets are usually found near a bird's nest, its roosting site or its feeding ground.

Left: A dissected eagle owl's pellet. The contents include bones and pieces of fur, hair and feathers.

Food is the most important thing in a bird's life, especially during the breeding season. When parent birds are feeding their young, they often have to adapt their diet as the chicks cannot digest anything hard; baby finches, for instance, eat insects not seeds.

Rook pellets contain a lot of vegetable matter such as stalks, grain husks and seed shells as well as small stones – or grit – that have been swallowed to help digestion.

Pellets

A bird often swallows things that it cannot digest, such as bits of bone, fur or husk. These collect and are pressed together to form a lump or pellet which the bird coughs up. The most familiar pellets belong to birds of prey and owls; many other birds produce pellets but because they are so small they are hard to find.

Pellets can be dissected and will provide valuable information about a bird's diet and feeding habits. To dissect a pellet, soak it in a dish of warm water for half an hour. Then, gently separate the contents using a long needle, remove them from the water with a pair of tweezers and leave them to dry.

Identification is fascinating. With the aid of a good reference book and a magnifying glass it is relatively easy to recognize the bones of certain small animals – like voles and fieldmice in an owl's pellet – but insect wingcases and seed husks are more difficult to name.

Senses

Birds have the same senses as human beings – smell, taste, touch, hearing, sight – but they have developed

Because a bird's eyes are so large there is little room in the skull for the muscles that move eyes up and down and from side to side. So, to keep objects in sight, birds have to turn their heads. Owls can turn their heads through 270 degrees – almost a full circle – and even upside down. Owls, like most birds of prey, have their eyes at the front of the head: this helps them to see ahead very clearly and locate prey more easily. But other birds have eyes at the side of the head: although they cannot focus very well, they can at least see in most directions at once and so keep a look-out for danger.

differently. The two most important by far are sight and hearing.

Birds have very large eyes in relation to head size, and this gives them keen vision for spotting enemies, finding a mate, keeping together in flocks and, very important, for feeding: an eagle can spot a rabbit two kilometres away, which no human would be able to do without the help of binoculars.

With their songs and calls, birds send all kinds of messages to one another. They also need their acute hearing to listen out for danger – like a cat. In the dark, owls even hunt by sound, locating a mouse by its noisy rustling.

Birds, like humans, see in full colour; this is important to them in identifying other birds, and perhaps in finding and recognizing food. Waterbirds have a transparent membrane which slides over their eyes when they are under water and allows them to see clearly there.

How Birds Behave

A bird needs an area where it feels safe and which it can call its own. This area is its territory and the bird will defend it fiercely against other birds of the same species. (Different species are not such a threat as they have distinct life styles: different diet, nesting sites and so on.) There are two main kinds of territory. One is used for nesting and feeding. The other kind is for nesting only.

Blackbirds, robins and most other garden birds have the first kind of territory. They claim exclusive nesting and feeding rights over a certain area of ground. Birds that use their territory for feeding as well as for nesting need an area large enough to provide food for them and their families. With small birds, like robins, a town garden is sufficient. A large bird of prey needs several square kilometres.

One method of studying territories is to mark on a large-scale map the sightings of a particular species. In this way the birdwatcher can build up an overall picture. Individual birds may return each year to the same territory, although the boundaries may be disputed.

A cock blackbird surveys its territory. Territories are usually defended by male birds; they use their brighter plumage and song to alert and warn off possible intruders. The strongest and most successful birds are able to take the best territories.

Seabirds that nest in colonies have very small territories – just the area around each nest which is usually within pecking distance of the next nest.

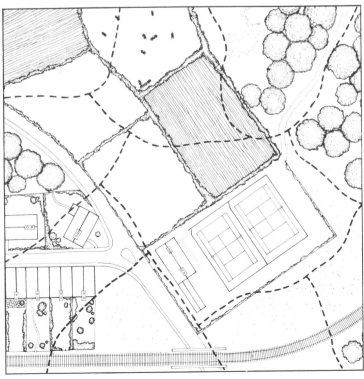

A pair of rooks feeding their young. During the breeding season, rooks greet each other at the nest by bowing and cawing. Although the female incubates the egg by herself, both parents help with feeding.

The courtship rituals of the great crested grebe are fascinating to watch. The birds often begin a courtship dance with elaborate head-wagging (1); the ritual may continue with everyday actions like preening (2); in the later stages of courtship one bird offers the other a fish (3); in the 'cat' display one grebe spreads its wings before the other (4); in the 'penguin' dance, the birds rise from the water, carrying weed in their beaks (5).

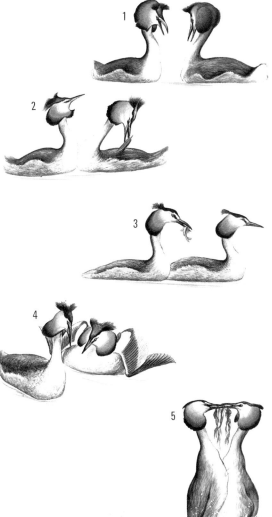

A great many birds have the second kind of territory: they guard their own nesting area but go beyond its boundaries to find food. Seabirds that breed in colonies behave in this way. As there are plenty of fish in the sea, there is no need for each bird to claim its own feeding ground; territory becomes just the nesting site – often not much bigger than the nest itself.

Finding a mate

Birds are constantly on the look out for danger and are suspicious of everything that moves – including other birds. They are even wary of their own species: because they all have the same diet they are competing for the same food.

At breeding time, however, the situation changes and birds must behave differently. Male and female birds have to form pairs and mate. They must usually stay together for the entire breeding season and work together at building a home and bringing up a family. While the male bird becomes tender and protective towards the female, it must also become more aggressive towards other males to stop them from breaking up the pair or from trespassing on their

A male red-breasted merganser performing its courtship display. The merganser is a freshwater duck that usually moves to the coast in winter.

The male black grouse or blackcock courts a female by raising a beautiful fan of white feathers. Because black grouse live on cold, high moors, they may begin to court when there is still snow on the ground.

territory. Yet, when the breeding season is over, the birds go back to their normal behaviour.

Chemical changes in the body allow birds to alter their behaviour for the breeding season. (These changes are probably controlled by the length of daylight.) But chemistry is not enough to attract a mate. Birds develop special songs, plumages, displays and dances to help them get together.

Courtship

As it is nearly always the male bird that courts the female, males tend to be more colourful. In spring, the male's feathers often become even brighter and many birds develop a special plumage just for the breeding season. The male chaffinch, for example, grows a blue-grey crown and the brambling goes deep black. One of the most spectacular breeding plumages belongs to the ruff. This marshland bird grows a broad collar of white, black or chestnut feathers round its neck as well as head plumes.

Several male birds use their colourful plumage in a special show or display. The ruff raises its collar and crown tufts, and parades in front of the female. Even dull-coloured birds have some form of display. The brown-grey dunnock, for example, flicks its wings as it hops about after a female.

Birds perform various other rituals as part of their courtship. In many species, including finches, the male feeds the female: this action not only increases

the bond between the two birds but probably serves as a rehearsal for feeding the incubating mate on the nest.

Some birds, among them members of the crow family and swans, pair for life and rarely leave each other's company. Others mate for the breeding season only.

Nests

Even before they are born, birds face danger. Eggs are fragile and break easily; they also taste good and are eaten by many animals. To protect their eggs and, later, their chicks, parent birds build nests.

In most species, the female bird chooses the nest site and sometimes builds the nest as well. But nest-building is hard work and often the two birds share it: swallows, for example, may have to make a thousand trips to collect enough material to construct their mud homes. The male bird rarely builds the nest by itself; the wren, however, builds several and then lets the female choose and complete one of them.

The majority of nests are open-plan, cup-shaped constructions sheltered by the sitting bird. For added protection, this type of nest is usually tucked away out of sight. Woodland birds, such as thrushes and finches, conceal their nests among the leaves of

Grebes build floating nests of weeds on lakes and rivers and anchor them to reeds to stop them drifting away. They put a rough roof of leaves and stems over the nest to protect the eggs.

house martin

woodpecker

nest box

reed warbler

great crested grebe

song thrush

long-tailed tit

robin

little tern

golden eagle

If there are not enough natural holes around, many birds – even tawny owls and barn owls – will breed quite happily in nest boxes. In woodland habitats, boxes must be protected from grey squirrels.

Left: A selection of nests. The house martin builds a mud nest under the eaves of houses; the woodpecker drills a hole into a tree trunk; nest boxes are popular with small birds, particularly tits; reed warblers construct their nests in riverside vegetation while grebes site theirs away from the bank but anchor it to reed stems; the song thrush has a typical open cup-shaped nest; the long-tailed tit's beautiful domed nest is woven from moss and spiders' webs; robins will make use of all sorts of strange objects as nest boxes; on a beach, the little tern's eggs become lost among the pebbles; the golden eagle returns to the same nest every year.

Instead of building their own nests, members of the falcon family, like this kestrel, often take over an empty crow's nest.

bushes and trees. Bright-coloured birds, like the bullfinch and linnet, hide among brambles and gorse; even if enemies do spot them, they are put off by the prickly thorns.

Many species build on the ground, but the nest and birds are so well camouflaged that they are almost invisible. On a shingle beach, the tern's egg looks just like another pebble. Other birds keep their eggs out of danger by nesting in inaccessible places. Seabirds often breed on isolated rocky islets or steep cliffs, while some birds of prey choose high mountain ledges.

The alternative to an open cup-shaped nest is an enclosed nest with a side entrance hole. Many birds build this kind of nest, including the magpie, wren, chiffchaff and the long-tailed tit – its amazing nest is a delicate woven ball of feathers, moss and spiders' webs. The house martin's mud nest, built against a wall, also forms a complete shelter.

Various birds give their eggs all-round protection without building a nest at all. Instead they use holes. Hollows in trees or crevices in walls and rocks provide nesting places for owls, starlings, jackdaws, tits, sparrows and many others. Kingfishers and sandmartins make tunnels in river banks while puffins and shearwaters choose holes in the ground – often empty rabbit burrows. In general, birds use existing holes but a few make their own, like the woodpecker which drills into tree trunks with its sharp beak.

Instead of building a new nest each season, some birds, such as swans and eagles, return to the same one year after year. Others, like kestrels and sparrowhawks, take over the nest of another bird rather than construct their own.

Eggs

Mammals – the animal group that includes human beings – keep their developing young inside the mother's body. But in most animal groups, the female lays eggs. Birds do this, and one or both parents incubate them until the young are born – that, is until they hatch.

The egg forms inside the mother bird. It contains the embryo – the baby creature at its very smallest – yolk and albumen. The yolk, bright yellow, is the embryo's food store while the albumen is an important food store and also acts as a cushion, protecting the embryo and the yolk inside the shell. The shell itself is a hard, thin layer of calcium carbonate (the same chemical compound as chalk and marble) and is porous so that the chick can breathe.

Most birds, except for some seabirds and birds of prey, lay more than one egg. In general garden and woodland birds, such as starlings, sparrows, finches and thrushes, lay about four or five eggs. Hole-nesters, like kingfishers, woodpeckers and owls have

The greenshank, a moorland bird, makes a rough nest on the ground in the shelter of a rock or fallen branch. Its eggs are creamy yellow with dark brown blotches.

The avocet folds its long legs carefully as it lowers itself on to the eggs to incubate them.

Most eggs, like the blackbird's, are oval. But some, like the tawny owl's, are round while the guillemot has pear-shaped eggs.

guillemot

blackbird

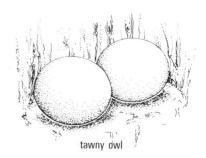

tawny owl

A cuckoo's egg in a reed warbler's nest. The female cuckoo waits until the other bird leaves its nest, then lays a matching egg and removes one of the original eggs – either by throwing it out or by swallowing it. When the foster bird returns it does not realize what has happened: there are the same number of eggs as before and they look quite alike, although the newcomer is rather larger.

The nest and eggs of the little ringed plover. The nest consists simply of a hollow made by the bird's body and the eggs – sandy with grey and brown spots – look like stones.

slightly larger clutches, from five to seven eggs. The most productive birds are ducks and gamebirds: the mallard, for example, can lay up to 16 eggs and the red grouse up to 17.

It takes several days to produce a clutch as the eggs are laid separately, with an interval of one or two days between each one. But in most cases, incubation does not start until the last one has been laid. By then, the mother bird has developed brood patches – patches of warm, bare skin that fit over the eggs. When the mother sits on the eggs, the heat from these patches helps the embryo to develop.

Incubation lasts about two weeks for most small garden and woodland birds, such as wrens, robins and sparrows. Larger birds, like magpies, jays and jackdaws, sit on their eggs for 17 or 18 days. Birds of prey, owls and seabirds take a month; and there are two ocean birds, the Manx shearwater and the fulmar, that incubate their eggs for seven or eight weeks. During incubation, the female bird may sit on the eggs all the time and be fed by its mate, or it may leave the nest to feed and let the male take over for a short stint.

Colours and sizes

Eggs come in various colours, ranging from pure white through pale greens and blues to darker shades of brown, red and black. They are often marked with speckles, streaks and blotches which help to camouflage them in the nest; this is especially true of ground-nesting birds. Birds that nest in dark holes, such as owls and woodpeckers, lay very pale or white eggs. Being hidden from view, there is no need for the eggs to be camouflaged; also, it is easier for the parent birds to spot light-coloured eggs in the dark gloom of the nest hole.

The eggs of each particular species are usually similar, although there may be slight differences in shade and markings. But the cuckoo's eggs have a tremendous range of colours and markings. This is because each female cuckoo selects a particular foster species for its young and lays an egg similar in appearance to the eggs of the foster bird.

In general, eggs are egg-shaped: oval with a large end tapering to a smaller one. Parent birds can easily turn this oval shape thus making sure that all sides receive warmth during incubation; oval eggs are also quite comfortable to sit on. Some eggs, like those of owls, are round; others are pear-shaped. Members of the auk family, such as guillemots and razorbills, lay pear-shaped eggs; if the eggs are accidentally knocked they spin round in a circle rather than roll off the narrow ledge.

Growing up

Breaking out of the egg is the first task that a bird has to face in life. It is not easy and can take from two hours to two days. The parent birds immediately remove – or eat – the broken shell as it is shiny white inside and could attract enemies to the nest.

Most birds are helpless at birth: they are blind and naked and rely totally on their parents. They lie at the bottom of the nest, huddled together for warmth and waiting to be fed. Whenever the nestlings hear their parents arrive (they cannot see them) they instinctively lift their heads and open their beaks wide. At night, one parent will cover the nest to protect its young from the cold.

Baby birds develop quickly. Within a few days they can see, and have a first coat of feathers. By the time they are two or three weeks old, many garden and woodland birds are able to fly; the hawfinch is airborne after only ten days. But some birds take much longer to learn to fly: swifts, for instance, need six weeks, barn owls ten weeks, and swans as many as fifteen weeks.

Once a bird begins to flutter, however hesitantly, it can get out of the nest and follow its parents. At first fledglings – baby birds that can fly – just wait on the ground or in a tree for their parents to bring food. (Never touch a fledgling, thinking it has been abandoned; its parents are probably nearby and will return to it as soon as you move away.) But as the days pass, they learn to get food for themselves by watching adult birds.

Even when they are confident about flying and feeding, young birds usually remain with their parents for a while to learn and practise new skills. Some bird families stay together throughout the summer. But others quickly break up. This happens with many small birds that have two or three broods a year. A young robin, for example has to fend for itself after only three weeks.

Not all birds are helpless at birth: some hatch in an advanced state with eyes open and a covering of downy feathers. Within a few hours they can run or swim and so leave the nest and go with their parents to find food. Many water birds and ground-nesting birds behave in this way. For instance, young woodcocks, born with a soft brown plumage, leave the nest immediately and mallard chicks take to the water just as quickly. In such cases, the parent birds

This cuckoo's foster parents are dunnocks. After hatching, the young cuckoo gets rid of all competition by throwing the dunnocks' babies and eggs out of the nest. The foster parents then spend all their time and energy on feeding the young cuckoo which grows so quickly that it soon fills the nest and dwarfs the parent dunnocks. Within three weeks, the cuckoo can fly and leaves the nest. The young cuckoo's penetrating cry for food may cause other birds, hurrying past with food for their young, to turn aside and feed it.

A robin feeds its greedy young with insect food. Whenever a parent bird approaches its nest, the young birds respond by opening their beaks wide. Baby birds develop quickly and require a lot of food: a brood of blue tits, for example, eat an average of 700 caterpillars a day.

keep a close watch on their young for several weeks.

The parent birds will take great risks to protect their young. They will peck and squawk to drive off intruders, and will sometimes pretend to be injured themselves to take a predator's attention away from the chicks.

The young bird usually has to wait to breed until the following year. Some large birds, however, take longer to mature. Owls, geese and various birds of prey must wait two years before breeding; several seabirds, including gulls, do not mature until their fourth year, while fulmars are often seven years old before they breed.

In many cases, immature birds have their own plumage: young robins are speckled brown, for example, and juvenile gulls have dull brown backs.

Birds rely on a regular food source in winter, and a well-stocked bird table will bring them to your garden. The greater the variety of foods that you give, the greater the number of different kinds of birds which are likely to visit it. But it is not a good idea to feed birds during the breeding season; natural foods, especially insects, are better for them and household scraps may even harm young birds.

Small tits, tree sparrows and pied flycatchers will use a nest box like this one. A box should have a removable lid, so that you can clean it out at the end of the breeding season. The floor should have a gap to allow water to drain away in wet weather. And the entrance hole should be only 28 mm in diameter – too small to let in house sparrows, who would otherwise take it over.

Attracting Birds

There are many ways in which we can improve our gardens to make them more attractive places for birds to feed and breed in. But before you start working out how to attract breeding birds to your garden, have a good look at it. Would it be a good place for birds to breed in? Is it big enough? Are there cats around? Are there sheltered places away from playing children? Breeding birds need a certain amount of peace and quiet, and playing children and prowling cats may well cause them to leave their nests.

Planting for birds

Most species of birds which breed in our gardens are woodland birds. This means that shrubby cover is important to them. They like a certain amount of undergrowth, such as bramble patches, and weed patches are very attractive to finches – even if they are unpopular with tidy gardeners. It is a good idea to pile up trimmings from hedges and bushes in a quiet corner, and train some bramble sprays to grow over them. This will give ideal cover for dunnocks and wrens, who can forage for food and even breed there. A mown lawn takes the place of the small open areas found in natural woodland.

The best garden for birds will have trees such as

elder, birch, hawthorn, alder and willow in it, because birds have adapted to feed on the insects which live on native trees like these. Berry-bearing trees and shrubs are very good for birds in late autumn and winter.

Building for birds

Put up a few nest boxes on tree-trunks and walls in your garden. You can buy nest boxes of several different types, or you can make them yourself. Never put them up where they will be exposed to the full sun; baby birds could be killed by the mid-day heat. Make sure that cats cannot get at the box. You can also make a simple bird table of a tray fixed to a post about 2 metres above the ground. At this height cats will not be able to jump on to it. You can fix a feeding tray on to a wall or hang it from a tree. Leave some gaps round the edge of the tray so that water can run away.

Feeding

Feeding birds is important in winter, when they may find it hard to get natural food. You must be sure to keep up a regular food supply, as the birds will come to rely on it. If they find no food in your garden, they may not be strong enough to fly on to search elsewhere.

Mixed feeds for wild birds can be bought in pet shops, or through advertisements in bird magazines. Household scraps are welcome winter food, including bread, cake, cheese, bacon rind, cooked potatoes and suet. Hang out nets full of peanuts, but make sure they are not salted ones, as salt is very bad for birds. If you can get a coconut, split it open and hang it up. When the shell is empty, you can fill each half with 'bird pudding' – a mixture of seeds and kitchen scraps bound with melted fat – and hang it upside down on a tree.

Special nest boxes for house martins, like the one above, can be bought; the birds live quite happily in colonies of mixed natural and artificial nests.

Birds need water as well as food, for bathing as well as for drinking. A small, shallow pond is useful, with stones in it on which the birds can perch. Water for birds is especially important in winter time, when many ponds are frozen over. You can easily make sure that a small garden pool is kept free of ice so that the birds can use it.

Conservation

Clearing land for building or for farmland has destroyed the habitats of many birds. Forests have been cut down and wetlands drained. Cultivating the land to grow crops, and grazing by farm animals, have destroyed much natural vegetation. As a result many forms of animal and plant life have become very rare, and some have even died out altogether.

Pollution has also had a devastating effect on wildlife. Chemical waste has killed off fish in rivers, and the birds that ate them, and insecticides sprayed on crops to protect them from pests have damaged the birds which fed on insects and on crops. More deliberately, egg collectors have raided the nests of rare birds to take their eggs, or to seize the chicks of falcons to be used for hunting. Hunters have killed birds for food and for their decorative feathers.

Gradually, people have become aware of the need to protect and save wildlife for the future. In many countries there are conservation organizations, some of them run by governments but many depending on money from their members. Some of them are small local trusts looking after small reserves where rare plants and interesting wildlife can live undisturbed. In Britain, Europe's largest voluntary conservation organization, the Royal Society for the Protection of Birds, runs more than 75 reserves and has over 280,000 members. There are laws to protect most wild birds, including all those in danger.

The water levels on low-lying fields which are likely to flood can be controlled by sluices. In winter the fields can be allowed to flood, and in spring the water is drained off again for the breeding season. Flood conditions are useful to flocks of wintering waterfowl, which can feed on the many plant seeds that are washed to the surface.

Managing a reserve
Nature reserves are not made by setting aside an area of land and just leaving it alone. A reserve needs

Far left: A large area of damp grassland is improved by making small pools. This is often done by blowing a hole with explosives. Left: Conservation workers clear dense thickets of rhododendron which are threatening the growth of natural woodlands. The shrubs are cut and burned, and the stumps are treated with a chemical which prevents new shoots from forming.

to be managed in rather the same way that a garden is looked after. Otherwise, some particularly thriving plants will take over and choke out other species that were there in the first place.

Carefully managed land can become a more interesting habitat for wildlife. The management may involve a certain amount of cutting down of bushes to open up areas where undergrowth can be established. Patches may have to be cleared in reed beds to make some open pools. And invading plants may have to be destroyed to bring about a better balance of vegetation. Even woodland may need some kind of management if they are to support the widest range of bird life. The traditional coppicing method of cutting trees almost down to the ground and letting shoots grow from the stump for a few years is very useful; it produces a wood with trees and bushes of several different ages and heights – suitable for the feeding and nesting of many kinds of birds.

Managing a habitat is quite a difficult job. Before any work is done, a detailed survey of the area must be carried out, so that a clear picture of the plant and animal life there can be built up. Then a plan can be made of the sort of plant and animal life that it is hoped to encourage there, and of the work to be done.

The avocet is one of conservation's success stories. It died out in Britain early in the 1800s, as a result of hunting and the disturbance of its marshland habitat. The Royal Society for the Protection of Birds has helped the bird to nest again in Britain, in special reserves. The avocet is the Society's symbol.

A Bird Calendar

The changing seasons bring with them many changes in the birds we see around us. Knowing what birds to look for, and where are the best places to look for them, at different times of year are key factors in successful birdwatching. Keen bird-watchers note down first and last sightings of summer and winter visitors, and compare one year with another. They make special visits to coastal areas where huge flocks gather during the spring and autumn migration periods. Even in towns and gardens, the seasonal changes are easy to see and hear.

The swallow arrives in spring, nests, and leaves in late summer to spend the winter in Africa. Britain lies at a great crossroads of bird migrations. Most summer visitors come from the south-west; in winter, wildfowl and waders fly south-east from Greenland and Iceland, or south-west from Scandinavia.

January
Lakes, reservoirs and estuaries are home for flocks of waterfowl and waders all winter through. Birds are almost all settled in one place, unless there is a snap of cold weather when large numbers of lapwings, skylarks, thrushes, wood pigeons and waterfowl will move to milder regions.

February
More and more gulls arrive on estuaries and inland reservoirs. Flocks of finches are feeding in farmyards and fields. Many birds are in song as they start to mark out their territories. Wildfowl are displaying and pairing up before they move north to their breeding grounds. Herons, crows and some garden birds begin to build their nests if the weather is fine.

March
Waders crowd the coasts and estuaries in ever greater numbers as birds arrive from farther south. The first wheatears, sand martins and chiffchaffs begin to arrive from the middle of the month onwards. More birds are singing, and the flocks of finches and buntings start to break up as the birds set up their own territories. Partridges and lapwings call and display.

April
The breeding season is now in full swing for many birds. Summer migrants are arriving in good numbers, and many other migrants are moving through the countryside on their journey farther north. The first cuckoos are heard and swallows arrive. By the end of the month, most winter visitors have flown on their way.

May
Many of the summer migrants are now breeding, and the countryside is full of song. Still more birds arrive. In the first half of the

month come the swifts. Finches journey along the coasts where rare migrants which have strayed from their route may also be found. Coastal cliffs are bustling with breeding seabirds.

June
By now the waders have almost deserted the estuaries. The main migrations have now finished, but rare strays can still be found along the coast. On the moorlands, curlew and golden plover are displaying. The summer visitors are nesting, while the young of resident birds are learning to fly. Lapwings are starting to flock and move away from the edges of moorlands.

July
Some waders are now coming back on to estuaries. Young seabirds are leaving the cliffs. Towards the end of the month, a few small migrant birds move along the coast. Most birds are now moulting, and are not singing much.

August
Flocks of moulting waterfowl gather on inland lakes, and shelduck have left to moult in Heligoland Bight. Migration is getting under way and large numbers of waders are passing through. Moorlands, deserted by the waders now the breeding season is over, are quiet. Many migrants of all kinds are found along the coast.

September
The numbers of waders passing through drops towards the end of the month. Waterfowl begin to gather on inland waters to spend the winter. Many small migrant birds are on the move. The first of the winter thrushes start to arrive on the east coast, and move inland.

October
Easterly winds bring with them large numbers of winter visitors, especially thrushes. A few strays from Central Asia turn up along east and south coasts, also blown in. Flocks of waterfowl are building up on lakes. Wintering waders are found in large numbers on estuaries. There are flocks of finches and larks in stubble fields and farmyards, and redpolls and siskins on alders and birches. Tawny owls start hooting again. By now, all summer visitors have left.

November
Redwings and fieldfares are stripping berries from the hedges. In good years, waxwings turn up along eastern coasts. Bramblings, often mixed with chaffinches, feed in flocks on fallen beechnuts. Thrushes, rooks, jackdaws and starlings form large roosts. Woodland birds gather into mixed flocks to roam through the trees.

December
Few birds are moving around now. They stay in their winter quarters unless cold weather forces them to fly to milder areas. Large numbers of gulls gather to roost on inland lakes and estuaries. Guillemots start to visit their breeding cliffs.

In autumn and winter, flocks of waxwings may arrive to feed on berries. They roam around in search of food, and fly off again as soon as spring arrives. These unusual birds have no particular homes, except during nesting, which takes place in Arctic regions. Flocks of them wander from place to place in search of food; they may be seen one year, and then not for a gap of several years.

Classifying Birds

There are some 8600 different species of birds in the world. Not surprisingly, several people have worked out different ways of grouping them together, and the most often used is the one we show here. It was put forward by Alexander Wetmore in 1930, and it is called the Wetmore Sequence. The birds are grouped together because they are similar in anatomy, structure and behaviour – though it may take a trained eye to see the likenesses!

International names

All birds, like other living organisms, have been given scientific names which come from Latin or Greek. These are used internationally. This is useful when dealing with ornithologists in other parts of the world. The bird known as the dunlin in Britain is called the red-backed sandpiper in North America; in France it is the *bécasseau variable*, and it has many other names in different parts of the world. But all over the world it will be known to ornithologists by its scientific name, *Calidris alpina*.

The first part of the name shows the genus to which the bird belongs, and the second its species. Birds of the same species can breed together and produce fertile young; birds of species which are closely related but cannot breed together are grouped in the same genus. The dunlin shares the genus *Calidris*

The brambling, *Fringilla montifringilla*, is a close relation of the chaffinch, *Fringilla coelebs*. In winter time flocks of mixed chaffinches and bramblings can be seen in Britain, but in spring the brambling flies north to breed in Scandinavia and Siberia.

Orders of Birds

GAVIIFORMES
Gaviidae (Divers: 4)

PODICIPEDIFORMES
Podicipedidae (Grebes: 5)

PROCELLARIIFORMES
Procellariidae (Shearwaters: 6)
Hydrobatidae (Storm Petrels: 3)

PELECANIFORMES
Sulidae (Gannets: 1)
Phalacrocoracidae (Cormorants: 3)
Pelecanidae (Pelicans: 2)

CICONIIFORMES
Ardeidae (Herons: 9)
Ciconiidae (Storks: 2)
Threskiornithidae (Ibises: 2)

PHOENICOPTERIFORMES
Phoenicopteridae (Flamingos: 1)

ANSERIFORMES
Anatidae (Ducks: 45)

ACCIPITRIFORMES
Accipitridae (Hawks: 27)
Pandionidae (Ospreys: 31)

FALCONIFORMES
Falconidae (Falcons: 10)

GALLIFORMES
Tetraonidae (Grouse: 5)
Phasianidae (Partridges: 7)

GRUIFORMES
Turnicidae (Hemipodes: 1)
Rallidae (Rails: 9)
Gruidae (Cranes: 2)
Otididae (Bustards: 2)

CHARADRIIFORMES
Haematopodidae (Oysterchaters: 1)
Recurvirostridae (Avocets: 2)
Burhinidae (Stone Curlews: 1)
Glareolidae (Pratincoles: 2)
Charadriidae (Plovers: 8)
Scolopacidae (Sandpipers: 32)
Stercorariidae (Skuas: 4)
Laridae (Gulls: 14)
Sternidae (Terns: 10)
Alcidae (Auks: 6)

The bullfinch, like the brambling, is a member of the finch family, the Fringillidae. Its Latin name is *Pyrrhula pyrrhula*, and as you can see it belongs to a different genus from the chaffinch and brambling. Its beak is stouter and shorter than that of the chaffinch, but its dancing flight, and woodland and garden habitat are similar.

with several other similar species, among them the little stint, which is *Calidris minuta*.

Sometimes birds of one species show small differences when compared with birds of the same species from a different place, although they can still breed together. These differences may call for the species to be divided into sub-species; and when subspecies are referred to, the name is given in three parts.

Families and Orders
Dunlins, stints and other members of the genus *Calidris* are waders. They are grouped with other less closely related waders in the family Scolopacidae. And a number of families is collected into an order. The order in which the dunlin is placed includes other birds of estuaries and shores, among them gulls, plovers, and avocets.

The table shows how European birds are grouped into orders, and then into families. It also shows the number of regular species in each family. More than half of the species belong to the order Passeriformes, or perching birds; other orders contain only one or two species.

Help!

There is usually little to be done for injured birds, unless they are only very slightly hurt or are simply exhausted by bad weather. An exhausted bird can be fed and kept warm and dry for a day or two, until it is lively enough to be released. Sometimes you may find a stunned bird by the roadside which has no obvious sign of injury. Pick it up and put it in a sheltered place nearby; it will soon recover if it has only been stunned.

Small birds with broken wings will never be able to fly properly again, so probably the kindest thing to do is to destroy them. But large birds, such as swans, can live for many years even if they cannot fly. It is worth strapping up an injured wing as shown below. A broken leg is little handicap except to a long-legged bird and it can be splinted. Minor wounds can be cleaned with soap and water (no detergent) but more serious injuries should be treated by a vet.

Unfortunately, a bird covered in oil is a fairly common sight on beaches today. Such a bird should be taken to a local society that helps animals, which will know what to do. Oiled seabirds can be cleaned, but this destroys the waterproofing in their feathers and they should be kept until they have moulted and grown new seaworthy feathers. The law does not allow you to keep wild birds in captivity and you must release any bird as soon as it is fit enough to go.

Above: Warm, soapy water and an old toothbrush can be used to remove oil from a seabird's feathers. A rubber band placed carefully around the tip of the bird's bill prevents it from pecking its helper.

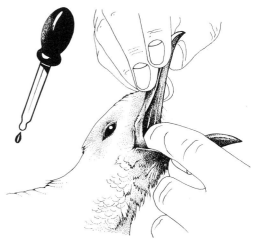

Above: Most injured wild birds have to be 'force-fed'. Open the bird's bill with your finger nails and push tiny pieces of food well down its gullet. Water can be given with a dropper. Make sure that you give the right kind of food – cake or biscuit for seed-eaters, mealworms or tinned catfood for insect-eaters. All birds like bits of hard-boiled egg.

Far left: Splinting a broken leg; the split shaft of a large feather is ideal for this. Bind the splint with sticky tape.

Left: Strapping up a wing; it should be strapped to the body in a folded position until it is healed.

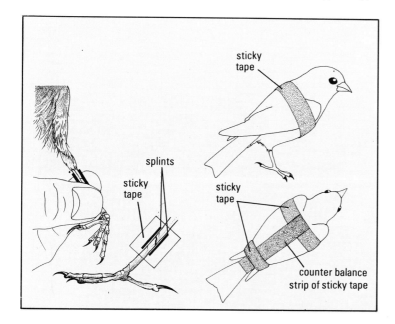

splints

sticky tape

sticky tape

sticky tape

sticky tape

counter balance strip of sticky tape

Books to Read

As you become interested in birds, you will need a small library of books to help you to recognize them and to learn about them. It is a good idea to have at least two field guides to help you check birds' identities. Then you will want other books about where and when to look for birds and their nests. Here are the names of a few books which you will certainly find helpful.

The Easy Way to Bird Recognition by John Kilbracken, published by Kingfisher Books.

A Field Guide to the Birds of Britain and Europe by Roger Tory Peterson, Guy Mountford and P. A. D. Hollom; published by Collins.

The Hamlyn Guide to Birds of Britain and Europe by Bertel Bruun and Arthur Singer; published by Hamlyn.

Illustrated Guide to Birds and Birdwatching by Neil Ardley; published by Kingfisher Books.

A Field Guide to Birds' Nests by Bruce Campbell and James Ferguson-Lees; published by Constable.

Where to Watch Birds by John Gooders; published by Deutsch.

The New Bird Table Book by Tony Soper; published by David and Charles.

Places to Visit

Some places are particularly good for watching birds, among them estuaries which are packed with birds all the year through. Among the best estuaries for watching waders (based on counts done by the British Trust for Ornithology) are Chichester Harbour in the south of England; Foulness in the south-east; the Wash in the east; Lindisfarne in the north; the Firth of Forth and the Firth of Clyde in Scotland; Morecambe Bay and the Dee estuary in the north-west; Burry Inlet in South Wales, and the Severn estuary in the west. Good places in Ireland include Strangford Lough, Lurgan Green, and Shannon-Fergus.

Find out about reservoirs near you; these are also splendid places for bird watching. Observatories are dotted round the coasts of Britain; The British Trust for Ornithology will send you a list. And find out about bird reserves. Among the best known are Minsmere in Suffolk, run by the Royal Society for the Protection of Birds, and the Wildfowl Trust's headquarters at Slimbridge in Gloucestershire. Your County Naturalists' Trust will also have reserves where you can watch birds. You may need a permit to visit a nature reserve; check first.

Societies to Join

One of the best ways of learning to be a good birdwatcher is to join a society. Your local public library should be able to give you a list of birdwatching groups in your particular area. Most societies organize field meetings in the summer, and indoor meetings on winter evenings when people are invited to give talks about birds, often illustrated with a film or slides. There are also the great national societies.

The Royal Society for the Protection of Birds The Lodge, Sandy, Bedfordshire, is more than just a bird protection society. It not only runs reserves but produces films and has set up local groups for birdwatchers. Its **Young Ornithologists' Club,** for people under 18, helps young birdwatchers to meet experienced watchers who will take them out on trips; it holds meetings and produces its own magazine.

The British Trust for Ornithology, Beech Grove, Tring, Hertfordshire was formed to bring birdwatchers together to share one another's observations. It organizes a nationwide ringing scheme, and a census of common birds.

Glossary

Not all these words appear in this book, but you may well come across them in other books about birds and their habits.

Abrasion The effect of wear on feathers, often showing in the markings about the edges of the wing. Feathers are worn away through abrasion.

Adult A bird that has reached its definitive plumage and is capable of breeding.

Albino Lacking pigment, through genetic abnormality or due to age or an accident. True albinos are rare; they are white with pink eyes and skin, but partial albinos, with white patches, may be seen.

Albumen The 'white' of an egg, which feeds and cushions the growing embryo.

Allopreening Term used when two birds preen each other.

Altricial Young birds that are hatched blind and naked; an alternative term is *nidicolous*.

Avian The class of animals known as birds are referred to in scientific terms as Aves. Anything to do with birds is *avian*.

Axillaries The feathers at the base of the underside of the wings – the 'armpit'.

Banding Another term for RINGING.

Barb Part of the vane of a feather.

Bib The part of a bird's plumage which lies just under its beak.

Bird of prey A bird that looks for animals to eat; this term is usually used for birds belonging to the orders Accipitriformes and Falconiformes, which include eagles, kites, hawks, falcons and ospreys. Owls, which belong to the order Strigiformes, are also birds of prey.

Breeding season The time when birds are building nests and raising their young, from early spring to late summer.

Brood Collective term for a nest of young.

Burrow A hole in a bank or in the ground where a bird nests; some birds use existing burrows (such as rabbit holes) and others make their own.

Call A short sound, different from its usual song, made by a bird usually to indicate danger or to contact another bird. Calls help keep a bird family together.

Cere Bare skin about the base of the bill, as in birds of prey.

Chick A bird that, while too young to fly, can leave the nest, and walk or swim.

Clutch The set of eggs that exists when a bird has finished laying and is incubating.

Cock A male bird.

Colony Birds gathered together in a group to breed.

Covey A collective noun for a party of partridges.

Crest A small group of feathers on the back or top of a bird's head, that can be raised or lowered.

Crown The top of a bird's head.

Decoy An artificial bird placed to attract wild birds, such as waterfowl, on to a pond, or a form of trap to catch waterfowl.

Dispersal The spreading-out of a bird population from a point of origin.

Display An activity of a bird during courtship, or while threatening off competitors. It may include making special attitudes, puffing out feathers and singing.

Diurnal Active during daylight hours.

Down Fluffy feathers covering a young bird, and next to the skin of adult birds under the main feathers.

Drift A term used to describe a shift by migrating birds away from their normal migration route; it is often caused by weather conditions.

Dust bathing Many birds take delight in 'bathing' in powdery soil. It is thought that this helps to free their plumage from parasites.

Eclipse plumage A state of plumage that male ducks moult into after the end of the breeding season; in *eclipse* they are dull-coloured and look like the females. The colourful male plumage is grown again in early winter.

Egg tooth A small projection on the beak of a baby bird which helps it to break out of its eggshell.

Embryo The developing bird inside the egg.

Eyrie The nest of a large bird of prey.

Fall A term used to describe the situation when a number of migrant birds is forced to land by bad weather.

Fledgling A young bird that can fly but has not yet left the nest.

Game bird A bird shot for sport, especially pheasant, partridge and grouse.

Gape The inside of the mouth and bill; in fledglings the gape may be brightly coloured to attract the attention of an adult bird returning with food.

Genus The scientific term for a group of closely related species.

Gizzard Part of the stomach of a bird.

Grit Small stones that are swallowed by the bird and held in the gizzard to help digestion.

Habitat The surroundings in which a bird is found, such as heath or woodland.

Hen A female bird.

Hide A construction (permanent or portable) from which a birdwatcher can look at birds without being seen himself.

Hybrid A cross between two species. It is fairly rare

in the wild, but often happens in captivity where birds are kept in unnaturally close conditions.

Immature A term applied to plumages other than fully adult.

Invasion A sudden expansion of a bird's range into areas where it is not normally found.

Introduced bird A kind of bird that has been brought to live in an area from elsewhere. Mandarin ducks, for example, have been brought from China to live in Europe.

Juvenile Name given to the first true covering of feathers a bird has after leaving the nest. In some birds, juvenile plumage may be seen as late as the following winter, in which case it may be referred to as 'first-winter'.

Latin names The classification names of birds are in a form of Latin because this can be understood throughout the world, whatever the local name of the bird.

Lek A display ground for certain species, such as black grouse and ruff.

Lure A form of bait used by falconers while training their birds, or an instrument used for imitating bird calls.

Migration The journeys that certain birds make each year between the areas where they breed and where they spend the winter.

Mimicry A bird's imitation of sounds made by other birds and incorporation of them into its own song.

Mobbing The chasing of birds of prey, crows and other predatory birds by smaller birds in an attempt to move them away from their territories.

Moulting The losing of old feathers and growing of new ones.

Nestling A young bird, living in the nest.

Nictating membrane A membrane which can cover the exterior of the eye, to clean or protect it. It is rather like a transparent third eyelid.

Nidicolous Another term for ALTRICIAL.

Nidifugous Another term for PRECOCIAL.

Nocturnal Active at night.

Observatory A special building for birdwatchers, in a place where interesting birds and particularly migrants are found. Birds are recorded by daily counts and ringing. Visitors can often stay there in simple accommodation provided they book in advance.

Oology The study of birds' eggs.

Orbital ring A ring of differently coloured feathers around the eye.

Ornithology The study of birds.

Palmate Having three toes connected by webs.

Peck order A social order developed by a group of birds living or feeding together, in which some birds dominate others; the dominant bird is at the top of the peck order.

Pectoral The breast region of a bird.

Pellet A lump of indigestible food matter ejected through a bird's mouth.

Plumage The feathers that cover a bird's body.

Precocial Young birds that are active soon after hatching and are covered in down. The alternative name is *nidifugous*. Domestic chicks and ducklings are good examples.

Preening The cleaning of the feathers with the beak or feet.

Primary feathers The large feathers at the end of a wing which, with the secondaries, are the most important feathers for flight.

Population The number of birds of any one kind living in a particular area.

Range The area within which a particular kind of bird is found. Its summer and winter ranges may be different.

Relict populations Isolated populations of a species that was probably more widespread at one time.

Ringing Also known as banding in North America. The study of birds by trapping them and placing small numbered rings on their legs. Much is learnt about migration, population, breeding success, survival rate, and life span by ringing.

Roost A place where birds sleep, either on their own or in groups.

Secondary feathers The large wing feathers in the wing's hind edge.

Song The arrangement of sounds or notes used by a bird (usually male) to attract its mate and to claim its territory. A bird may have several different songs.

Species A term used in classifying birds (and other animals). Birds of the same species breed among themselves and produce fertile young. Species which are closely related are grouped in the same genus.

Subspecies Birds which belong to the same species and can breed together, but which are slightly different, perhaps through living in different areas.

Talons The strong, sharp claws of a bird of prey.

Territory The area which a bird or a pair of birds consider their own during the breeding season, or as a winter feeding area. A bird will defend its territory against other birds of the same kind which enter it.

Waterfowl Birds which live by water such as ducks, geese and swans, coots and moorhens.

Wildfowl Ducks, geese and swans.

Wingbars Bands of white or colour on the wings.

Vagrant A wandering bird found far outside its normal range.

Zygodactyl Having two toes directed forwards and two back.

Index

Entries in *italics* indicate an illustration.

ACKNOWLEDGEMENTS

Cover: Ardea Photos; 6 left P. Morris, right B. Hawkes; 7 left B. Hawkes, right Michael Chinery; 8 Eric and David Hosking; 10 RSPB Young Ornithologists' Club; 11 S. Madge; 14 S. Madge; 15 top S. Madge; 16 top right Brian Hawkes; 19 top Eric and David Hosking; 18 Brian Hawkes; 19 top Eric and David Hosking; 20 S. Madge; 21 top left Brian Hawkes, bottom right S. Madge; 22 left N.H.P.A.; 23 Brian Hawkes; 24 S. Madge; 25 bottom Brian Hawkes; 26 Brian Hawkes; 27 S. Madge; 28 Brian Hawkes; 29 N.H.P.A.; 30 Brian Hawkes; 31 top left and bottom Brian Hawkes, top right Eric and David Hosking; 32 top P. Morris; 33 top Brian Hawkes; 34 N.H.P.A.; 35 Brian Hawkes; 36 top left Eric and David Hosking; 37 bottom right N.H.P.S./S. Dalton; 38 top Eric and David Hosking, bottom P. Morris; 39 N.H.P.A.; 40–41 P. Morris; 40 bottom Brian Hawkes; 42 Brian Hawkes; 43 Brian Hawkes; 44 Brian Hawkes; 45 Brian Hawkes; 46 top left Brian Hawkes; 47 bottom right Brian Hawkes; 48 Brian Hawkes; 49 N.H.P.A.; 50 bottom right Brian Hawkes; 51 bottom left Brian Hawkes; 52 Brian Hawkes; 53 N.H.P.A.; 54 Brian Hawkes; 55 Brian Hawkes; 56 bottom left Frank Blackburn/Nature Photographers; 57 Eric and David Hosking; 58 Brian Hawkes; 59 Brian Hawkes; 60 top left Brian Hawkes; 61 N.H.P.A.; 62 top S. Madge, bottom Brian Hawkes; 63 N.H.P.A./A. Barnes; 64 Brian Hawkes; 65 top Brian Hawkes, bottom S. Madge; 67 bottom N.H.P.A.; 68 top Eric and David Hosking, bottom Brian Hawkes; 69 top P. Morris, bottom Brian Hawkes; 70 S. Madge; 71 top Brian Hawkes; 72 Brian Hawkes; 73 Biofotos; 74 S. Madge; 75 top S. Madge, bottom Brian Hawkes; 76 Biofotos; 77 P. Morris; 78 bottom left N.H.P.A.; 79 right Bruce Coleman; 80 Brian Hawkes; 81 John Markham/Bruce Colemen; 82 top P. Morris, bottom Brian Hawkes; 83 top Brian Hawkes, bottom P. Morris; 84 centre P. Morris; 85 top P. Morris; 86 top S. Madge, bottom F. Greenaway/Natural Science Photos; 87 top Eric and David Hosking, bottom Brian Hawkes; 88 N.H.P.A.; 89 bottom Brian Hawkes; 90 Brian Hawkes; 91 top N.H.P.A./S. Dalton, bottom Brian Hawkes; 92 left Brian Hawkes; 93 top Brian Hawkes, bottom left S. Madge; 94 top Brian Hawkes; 95 top N.H.P.A., bottom Brian Hawkes; 96 left Brian Hawkes; 97 top Brian Hawkes, bottom Eric and David Hosking; 98 top Brian Hawkes, bottom left Bruce Coleman; 99 top Brian Hawkes, bottom S. Madge; 101 Eric and David Hosking; 102 Brian Hawkes; 103 Brian Hawkes; 104 S. Madge; 105 Eric and David Hosking; 107 top Brian Hawkes, bottom N.H.P.A.; 108 Eric and David Hosking; 109 N.H.P.A.